T0024790

Writing Club II:

A Year of Writing Workshops for Grades K-2

by Carmella Van Vleet

LINWORTH LEARNING

Activities & Resources From the Minds of Teachers

Dedication:

To all the wonderful people at Oak Creek Elementary in Lewis Center, Ohio.

And with special thanks to Barbara Eisenhardt,
the artist who did the fantastic illustrations for both Writing Club books.

Library of Congress Cataloging-in-Publication Data

Van Vleet, Carmella.
  Writing club II : a year of writing workshops for grades K-2 / Carmella
Van Vleet.
     p. cm.
  Includes bibliographical references and index.
  ISBN 1-58683-188-7 (pbk.)
  1. Language arts (Primary)--Activity programs. 2. English
language--Composition and exercises--Study and teaching (Primary) 3.
Education, Primary--Activity programs. I. Title. II. Title: Writing club
two. III. Title: Writing club 2.
LB1528.V36 2005
372.62'3--dc22

                              2005005428

Published by Linworth Publishing, Inc.
480 East Wilson Bridge Road, Suite L
Worthington, Ohio 43085

Copyright © 2005 by Linworth Publishing, Inc.

All rights reserved. Purchasing this book entitles a librarian to reproduce activity sheets for use in the library within a school or entitles a teacher to reproduce activity sheets for single classroom use within a school. Other portions of the book (up to 15 pages) may be copied for staff development purposes within a single school. Standard citation information should appear on each page. The reproduction of any part of this book for an entire school or school system or for commercial use is strictly prohibited. No part of this book may be electronically reproduced, transmitted, or recorded without written permission from the publisher.

ISBN: 1-58683-188-7

5 4 3 2 1

Table of Contents

Table of Contents Continued

Reproducibles for handouts or transparencies.

Welcome to Writing Club II Workshops

This book contains eight writing workshops designed especially for students in kindergarten through second grade. Each workshop includes an introduction, list of materials and five writing activities. Each activity has a list of three to five books you might want to explore or use when doing the lesson. Though the books are not necessary to complete the activity, using them will add to the lesson and increase learning opportunities. In addition, each workshop includes a suggestion for a special transitional item for children to pull out at the beginning of each Writing Club lesson. For example, to help "stir up fun" in Food Fun, the students get a paper spoon to decorate.

Workshops can be done in any order. They are all equally challenging. The lessons within the workshops, however, are arranged in cumulative order. The fifth and final lessons in each workshop are designed as enrichment activities, which are great to challenge eager or older writers.

Even though each activity meets numerous curriculum standards and benchmarks, the main goals for language arts are listed at the beginning of each lesson. By their very nature, each activity aims to improve a basic skill such as using inventive and conventional spelling, writing in complete sentences, using proper sentence format, and properly forming and spacing letters. Many lessons also provide students with the chance to illustrate, display, or share their work.

There are often several ways to expand each lesson into other areas of the curriculum, such as geography, history, math, and science. Teaching tips are included with each activity.

You should plan on using about 30 minutes to complete each lesson. Chances are good, though, students will be having so much fun, they'll beg to keep writing!

Some Thoughts about Young Writers

When I was teaching in the classroom, I wanted to share my love of writing with my young students. Unfortunately, I quickly discovered there was little out there for kindergartners, first graders, and second graders that was really fun and challenging. In order to have what I wanted and needed in my classroom, I did what many teachers do—I made up my own material! Many of the lessons in this book are ones I created to meet specific curriculum goals or to nurture a particular interest of my students. Some of them were created for other classrooms. For example, when my son's first grade teacher asked me to come visit, I asked about skills they were working on at the time. (They were doing adjectives.) The lesson, "Lucy's Birthday," in which children are asked to describe a birthday gift, was the result.

I've always enjoyed working with writers of all ages, but I especially enjoy working with the youngest of writers. They are thrilled to *finally* be in school and are eager to master the skills necessary to join the rest of the "reading and writing world." Their enthusiasm is contagious! Here are a few things I've learned over the years from watching and working with kindergartners and first and second graders.

1. Young children are better writers than we sometimes think they are.

Many people, in my opinion, don't give beginning writers enough credit for being the truly enthusiastic and capable storytellers they are. It's been my experience that even children in kindergarten are able to grasp concepts such as character development, setting, mood, point of view, and author word choice.

Take every opportunity to point these things out while reading aloud to them. Ask them things such as, "Why do you think the author used this word here? Why do you think the main character acted that way? What kind of mood or feeling is the author trying to create?" Teach them to be observant readers and their own writing will improve.

2. Young writers like shorter lessons and lessons that draw on their own experiences.

While younger writers certainly have the ability to revise their work, they seem to be more successful with shorter assignments than with longer projects. (There are, of course, times when it's desirable to have children take the time to revise their writing.) Shorter assignments give quick payoffs. By this I mean children are able to write, illustrate, and publish (in some format) their work in a short amount of time. This short turnaround time helps young writers share their enthusiasm for the assignment with other classmates and parents. I call this the "Look what I did today!" effect. If writing is considered something fun, children will keep doing it.

Young writers also benefit from lessons that draw on their own experiences. Children, like adults, like to "write what they know." Familiar is good. Children are more confident writers when they see they have something of real value or experience to share. This is why Writing Club is filled with kid-friendly activities that deal with things like birthdays, lost teeth, favorite foods, and toys.

3. Young writers love (and need) to illustrate their writing.

Children who are decoding print frequently use visual cues. Because pictures are useful tools, giving young writers plenty of opportunity to illustrate their own work is important. Not only will students be able to remember their writing better, they'll be able to expand on their stories, poems, and other writings. (Writing a story that's a whole page long—gulp!—isn't nearly as intimidating as drawing a story that fills a whole page.) Many times, illustrating can also help young writers better organize their thoughts, which also makes orally sharing their work easier.

4. Young writers need to write every day.

Good writing skills, like reading skills, are essential across the curriculum. The more children write, the more comfortable they will become with the process. And writing *is* a process. Unlike subjects like math or science, writing has no "right answer." It is a series of starts and stops. It begins with a step forward and then a step backward. It requires time to think and discuss ideas. It requires time to write and then time to rewrite. By writing each day, children learn and practice important skills and gain confidence in their growing abilities. Even something as simple as writing a response to a "Today's Question" or writing in a journal, can help children see themselves as real writers.

5. Young writers need a writing center in their classroom.

Just as important as a special area to cozy up with a book is a place to let your creative juices flow on paper. Your writing center doesn't have to be fancy. A table and chairs with a bit of storage area will work. Different things inspire different writers, so fill the space with a wide variety of materials. Some of things you might consider for the writing center include: lined paper, unlined paper, drawing paper, construction paper, pre-made blank books, note cards, card stock, envelopes, stickers, markers, gel pens, pencils, colored pencils, ballpoint pens in a variety of colors (children really seem to love those four-colors-in-one-pen kind!), crayons, rhyming dictionaries, thesauri, rulers, and a tape recorder so kids can dictate a story or note an idea. I always like to include clipboards, too. Some children prefer finding their own writing space, and clipboards give them the freedom they need to move away from the table.

As far as writing prompts go, keep them simple. Story starters that you or the children have written, interesting pictures you've cut out from the newspaper, or intriguing newspaper headlines work great. Another super thing to have, if you can get your hands on them, is a collection of old book jackets. You can also create an "Ideas I *Can* Use" can. To do this, simply write words (or phrases) on slips of paper and put them in an old coffee can. Encourage students to use the can when they need a topic.

Happy writing!

Workshop Overview:
Me and My Family

It's only natural to write about what you know and this is especially true for the youngest of writers. Children often have great stories about their lives and this workshop celebrates those things that make them unique, such as their names and funny family adventures.

The main goals of this workshop are to give students practice researching, writing to give information, and re-telling stories. Much of the information students will research will come from parents or other family members, which also provides a wonderful opportunity for child and family to bond!

To get students into the right frame of mind (or is it the *write* frame of mind?), give each child a star—just like the ones movie and television stars have on their dressing room doors!

Writing activities	Materials and handouts *(one copy for each student)*
My Great Name!	Dressing Room Star File folders (one for each student) Baby name books (several for whole class use, optional)
How I Got My Name	My Name
Timeline of My Life	Drawing paper
Family News	The Family News Newspaper Newspapers or interesting headlines cut from the newspaper (optional)
My Funny Family	Katie's Crunchy Potato Salad transparency

Me and My Family
My Great Name!

Benchmarks/Standards covered:
- Identify initial consonant or vowel sound in words.
- Add/use descriptive words and details in writing.
- Produce informal writings (such as poems).
- Publish writing samples for display or sharing with others.

Books to explore:

The First Thing My Mama Told Me by Susan Marie Swanson (Harcourt Children's Press, 2002)
Mommy Doesn't Know My Name by Suzanne Williams (Houghton Mifflin, 1996)
My Name Is Yoon by Helen Recorvits (Farrar, Straus and Giroux, 2003)
A My Name is Alice by Jane Bayer (Puffin Books, reprint 1987)
Andy That's My Name by Tomie dePaola (Aladdin, 1999)

Discussion:

Start out with this riddle: What do you have that other people use all the time but that you don't use very often? Your name!

Today, we're going to use our names to write a poem called an acrostic. Acrostics use the letters of a word to come up with other words that describe it. For example, let's write an acrostic for a made-up girl named Kaitlin. (Be sure to write the name horizontally and the descriptive words or phrases underneath each letter. Use the following example or solicit responses from the students. K—kind. A—always smiling. I—in the 1st grade. T—takes swim lessons. L—long, brown hair. I—interested in animals. N—nice.) Words that describe are called adjectives. What are some other adjectives that start with the letters in Kaitlin's name we could use to describe her? Since we're making her up, we can make her be any way we want her to be! For example, if we wanted to be silly we could make the "K" stand for kooky or the "L" stand for lives at the zoo!

(Give each child a vanilla or light-colored file folder that's been cut in half horizontally. If a student has a long name, he or she may need two folders taped together.)

Now it's your turn:

Here's what to do: First, write your name in big letters. Make sure there are three fingers of space between each letter. When you're done, carefully cut between each letter all the way until you get to the fold. Now, you can lift each letter flap and write a descriptive word or phrase that begins with the letter.

Reminders for student writers:

- Try to think of things about yourself that might surprise people. Do you have a special talent or nickname? Have you been some place unusual?
- If you get stuck, ask a classmate to give you an idea or use the dictionary.

Teaching tips:

- This format is a great way to recycle old file folders and is especially easy for younger students who often have a hard time "lining up" columns or writing in a straight line.
- Early writers can cut out old magazine pictures of things they like that start with each letter of their name.
- Encourage students to use this kind of acrostic for other words besides their names. It's a fun way to learn new science or social studies vocabulary words.

Dressing Room Star

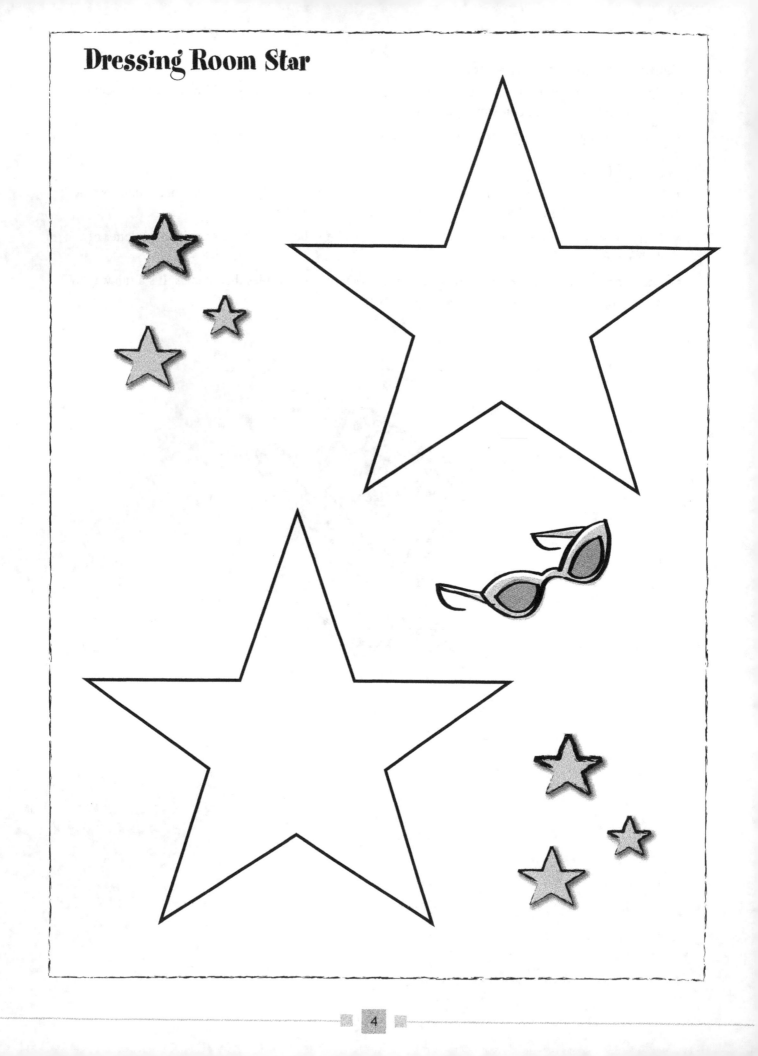

Me and My Family
How I Got My Name

Benchmarks/Standards covered:
- Recognize and print first name.
- Utilize appropriate searching techniques to gather information from a variety of locations.
- Report information to others.
- Identify and complete rhyming words and patterns.

Books to explore:

Best Baby Name Book in the World by Bruce Lansky (Meadowbrook, re-issued 1984)
The Name Jar by Yangsook Choi (Knopf Books for Young Readers, 2001)
Tikki Tikki Tembo illustrated by Blair Lent (Henry Holt and Co., re-issued 1989)

Discussion:

Your name is very special. It is one of the first presents you ever received and is a part of what you makes you, you! Have you ever wondered how you got your name? Who gave it to you? Does it mean anything special? How did you get your middle name? Do you have nickname? How did you get it?

When writers want to find something out, they research the topic. To do this, they might look up information in a book, ask other people questions, read, or visit a place. Can you think of any other ways somebody could find out information about a topic? (Responses might include watching a documentary, talking to an expert, searching the Internet.) Usually, writers begin with what they already know and then make a list of other things they'd like to find out about their topic.

Today, we're going to research our names. To begin with, we're going to start by writing down, or recording, all the things we already know. Next, we'll begin to research those things we don't know.

Now it's your turn:

(Give each student an All About My Name worksheet.) Take a look at the worksheet. Are there things you already know about how you got your name? How could you find out, or research, the information you don't know? (Responses might include: asking parents or grandparents, looking in a baby scrapbook, watching home videos. If possible, make a dictionary or rhyming dictionary available along with a baby name book.) Fill in what you can.

Reminders for student writers:

If you don't know the answer, leave it blank for now. You can research the answer later. (Send home worksheets as homework and encourage students to bring them back to share.)

When you're finished filling in the blanks, go to the top of the page, write your name, and decorate it if you'd like. Get creative!

Teaching tips:

- Consider holding a special Name Awards ceremony where you give each child an award such as: Longest Name, Most Unique Name, Most Unusual Story Behind the Name, Easy-to-Rhyme-With-Name, and so forth. (Older students can make up their own Name Award.)

- Make a class graph, "How many students like their name?"

- Have the students use the school directory to research the most common names in the school.

- Consider buying several used copies of a baby name book (or asking parents to donate their old ones).

All about My Name

My name:_____.

My nickname:_____.

The person who gave me my name:_____.

He or she picked this name because_____

_____.

Do I like my name?_____.

My name means:_____

_____.

Words that rhyme with my name:_____

_____.

Me and My Family
A Timeline of My Life

Benchmarks/Standards covered:
- Arrange events in sequential order.
- Connect what is heard to prior knowledge and experience.
- Write moving left to right.
- Name and label objects.

Books to explore:

Sarah Morton's Day: A Day in the Life of a Pilgrim Girl by Kate Waters (Scholastic, 1993)

The Man Who Walked Between the Towers by Mordicai Gerstein (Roaring Books, 2003)

When I Was Little: A Four-Year-Old's Memoir of Her Youth by Jamie Lee Curtis (Joanna Cotler, 1993)

Discussion:

When a writer writes about his or her own life, the story is called an autobiography. Many times, the first thing a writer does before he or she begins an autobiography is to create a timeline. A timeline is a very useful tool that helps you keep track of when things happened. (If your classroom uses a posted schedule, point out to students that a timeline is kind of like their schedule.) Timelines have a beginning and an ending and at least one thing in the middle. (Draw a line on the board or overhead and fill in appropriately, marking each highlight with a short, vertical line.) Let's try to create a timeline of our day so far. Where should be begin? (At the time the morning bell rang.) Where should we end? (At the time "Writing Club" began.) What important things or events happened in between the start of our day and now? (Responses might include, recess, lunch, music, or art class.)

(Draw another line.) Today, we're going to make a timeline of our lives. Here's one way the timeline of my life might look. (Start with your birthday and end with the current date and fill in several highlights of your life.)

Now it's your turn:

(Give each child a piece of paper to draft a timeline.)

Turn your paper on its side and draw a line. Start with your date of birth on the left side of the line. On the far right side of the line, put today's date. Next, spend a few minutes thinking about what you'd like to include in your timeline. What are some of the things you remember the most? Was breaking your arm memorable? Going to an amusement park? Are there any *important* dates to include, such as a brother or sister being born or your family moving? If you don't know the exact date of when something happened, fill in how old you were when something happened on the timeline.

Reminders for student writers:

- Remember, you don't need to fill in *everything* that has ever happened to you!
- If you'd like to spice up your timeline, you can draw some illustrations to go with a few of the special events of your life.

Teaching tips:

- Ask students to interview their parents for the dates (or ages) of milestones like their first step or word.
- Have older students include important dates in history along their timeline to tie-in social studies.
- Make a class timeline highlighting special days such as fieldtrips, vacation days, class birthdays, or lost teeth.

Me and My Family
Family News

Benchmarks/Standards covered:
- Recognize the defining characteristics and features of different types of literary forms and genres.
- Deliver formal and informal presentations recalling an event or personal experience that convey relevant information and descriptive detail.
- Rewrite and illustrate writing samples for display and for sharing with others.

Books to explore:

Deadline!: From News to Newspaper by Gail Gibbons (HarperCollins, 1987)
The Furry News by Loreen Leedy (Holiday House, 1993)
Fairy Tale News by Colin Hawkins (Candlewick Press, 2004)

Discussion:

Who knows what a journalist does? A journalist is someone who writes articles for a newspaper. Journalists report the news and other important things that are going on in a community. Can you think of some things journalists might write about? (Responses might include: a new store opening, a community event, a profile of a community member, a crime. If possible, bring in several newspapers for students to look through.) What are some other things you might find in a newspaper? (Responses might include: comics, weather reports, letters to the editor.)

Journalists write non-fiction. This means they write about things that have really happened instead of things that have been made up. They tell us the who, what, why, where, and how of a story.

Let's try writing a news story about a school activity. Can you think of something interesting to write about? (As a class, write a three or four sentence long story about a field trip or other classroom adventure on the board or overhead. Be sure to solicit *what* happened, *when* it happened, and *who* was involved. Add more details if you and the students wish to do so. Include a headline.)

Now it's your turn:

Today, you'll get the chance to be a journalist. We're going to write a story about something that happened in your family. (Hand each child The Family News Newspaper worksheet.)

Spend a few minutes thinking about something important or interesting that has happened in your family. Maybe a new brother or sister joined your family. Maybe you and your family went on a vacation. Maybe your family eats at a favorite pizza shop every week.

Next, write a short news story. Be sure to include the important details: what happened, when it happened, and who was involved. If you want to add how or why the event happened or other details, you can.

When you are finished, write a headline to go along with your story. Your headline should tell your reader a little bit about your story.

Reminders for student writers:

- Don't forget to add a few details. Details make a story interesting! Just make sure all the details are true because we are writing non-fiction.
- When you're done with the story, go back and draw a picture to go along with the news report. Make sure the picture tells your reader something about the story.

Teaching tips:

- Make a graph of how many students get or read the newspaper each day.
- Cut out interesting or funny headlines and bring them in. Older students might enjoy coming up with their own stories for the headlines.
- Extend this activity by writing a classroom newsletter for students to take home. Assign students or groups of students to a certain "beat" such as science, math, or recess.
- Begin each Monday by writing a class "Weekend News" report.

The Family's News Newspaper

Today's date:

Me and My Family
My Funny Family

Benchmarks/Standards covered:
- Connect prior experiences, insights, and ideas to those of a speaker.
- Organize writing to include a beginning, middle, and an end.
- Include transitional words and phrases.

Books to explore:

If Roast Beef Could Fly by Jay Leno (Simon and Schuster Children's Publishing, 2004)
Imogene's Antlers by David Small (Dragonfly Books, 1988)
Playhouse by Robert Munsch (Cartwheel Books, 2003)

Discussion:

Today, I have a funny story to share with you. (Share a story about something funny that happened to you as a child or as a grown-up.) Here's a funny story that happened in another family. (Put up Katie's Crunchy Potato Salad transparency and read together as a class.)

You may have noticed the example used a few special words. (Underline or circle the words *first, next, then, finally,* and *afterwards*.) These words are called transition words. Transition words are words that help a reader get from one part of the story to another. They help keep a story moving smoothly from its beginning to its middle to its ending. (If there's time, read the example without the transition words so students can hear the difference.) There are many, many words that can be used as transition words. But these are the five we'll be using today. (Write the words on the board or simply leave up the transparency.)

Now it's your turn:

All families have a funny story to tell, a story that always makes family members laugh. What's the funniest thing that has happened to you or to someone in your family? Did your mom go on vacation and forget her toothbrush after she reminded everyone else a dozen times to bring their toothbrushes? Did you tell a joke and make your older brother blow milk out of his nose? Did you and your cousin accidentally buy each other the exact same birthday card? Today, you'll get the chance to write your own funny, family story.

Begin by finding a partner. Take turns with your partner telling your funny story. (Re-telling a story first often helps students organize their thoughts.) Afterwards, write your story down on paper. Be sure your story has a beginning, middle, and an ending. To make your story smoother, be sure to include at least two of these transition words. (You can challenge older students to use more.) You might be surprised you do that without even thinking about it!

Reminders for student writers:

- Remember to think of others' feelings. Someone falling down might be funny, but someone falling down and getting hurt may not be.

13

- Also, it's okay to write about an embarrassing moment if it happened to you, but don't share someone else's embarrassing moment unless you know he or she wouldn't mind. If the story has been told lots of times and the other person doesn't get angry or sad, he or she probably wouldn't mind if the story was told again!

Teaching tips:

- Keep a class list of transition words students have come across in their reading.
- A class anthology of funny, family stories makes a great gift for parents.

Katie's Crunchy Potato Salad

Katie's family was planning a big, family picnic. There was a lot of work to be done. Mom was very busy and asked Katie to help.

"Katie, could you please make the potato salad? Everything you need is on the table."

"Sure, Mom," Katie said.

First, she got a big bowl and a spoon. Next, Katie put in the hard-boiled eggs, the mayonnaise, celery pieces, and mustard. Then, she put in the potatoes her mother had diced up. Katie stirred all the ingredients together and put the salad in the refrigerator.

Finally, it was time for the big picnic! Katie was excited. She had never made potato salad before and hoped everyone liked her dish.

Dad was the first one to try the Katie's potato salad. *Crunch!*

Next, Katie's brother tried the salad. *Crunch!*

Then Katie's mom tried a forkful. *Crunch!*

"Oh, no!" Katie's mom said, "I forgot to cook the potatoes!" Everyone laughed, even Mom.

Afterwards, Dad ran to the store to buy some potato chips. "At least these are *supposed* to be crunchy!" Katie said.

Workshop Overview:
Blast-Off!

Looking up into the night sky can certainly be inspiring. In this workshop, students will get the opportunity to take an imaginary trip to the stars aboard a space shuttle and rocket into fun and learning!

Once "in space," young writers will use similes and adjectives to describe their journeys in journals and letters home. They will also get the chance to write an ode to the moon and learn about and create their very own constellations.

Because we will be traveling into galaxies far away, students are each given a Space Traveler's ID badge to decorate and use while participating in this workshop.

Writing activities	Materials and handouts (one copy for each student)
Blast-Off!	Space Traveler's ID badge Space Journal page
Earth from Space	Earth worksheet
Good News/Bad News	Writing paper
Ode to the Moon	Ode to the Sun transparency Drawing paper (optional)
Constellation Creations	Small star stickers (a dozen per student) Black or navy construction paper Orion transparency

Blast-Off!
Blast-Off!

Benchmarks/Standards covered:
- Produce informal writings (such as journal pages).
- Identify words from text that appeal to senses.
- Use supporting details to identify and describe setting.

Books to explore:

Mr. Brown Can Moo, Can You? by Dr. Seuss (Random House Books for Young Readers, 1996)
Click, Clack, Moo: Cows That Type by Doreen Cronin (Simon & Schuster, 2000)
Whoosh! Went the Wish by Toby Speed (Putnam Publishing Group, 1997)

Discussion:

Let's read these words together. (Point to these words you've written on the board: buzz, hiss, sizzle, whoosh, screech, boom, click.) How are these words alike? They all have to do with sound! They are also words that make their own sound. Listen. (Read the words again, exaggerating the sound.) Can you think of any other "sound words?" (Record students' responses on the board.)

Writers use sound words to help readers feel as if they are really at a certain place. What are some places that have a lot of sounds? (Responses may include: airport, amusement park, the school cafeteria, a playground.) Another place where there are a lot of sounds is at a launch pad! Has anyone ever seen a rocket or space shuttle take off or watch one on television? What did you hear? Let's list some the sounds we might hear if we were there. (Record answers, which may include: the countdown, the roar of the engines, the crowd cheering, the blast-off.)

Now it's your turn:

Today, we are going to become space travelers! Let's pretend that we are getting ready to blast-off and then climb higher and higher in space. Since our families and friends can't come with us, let's write about our trip so they will know what it was like. (Students may pretend from their seats or create a space shuttle "set" by moving their chairs, painting large cardboard boxes, turning off the classroom lights etc. After students have lifted off and entered "space," ask them to put on their gravity boots and find a place to sit and write. Hand out the Space Journal page.)

Now, that we have a few minutes, let's write about what it was like to blast-off and what it's like to be and work in space.

Reminders for student writers:

- Don't forget to add sound words to your journal.
- Think of your other senses, too. What do you *see* in space? Do you *smell* anything? What does it *feel* like to float in space? How does the food *taste*?
- Write about how you felt during lift off. Were you scared? Excited? Did your seat rumble?

Teaching tips:

- Older students can write letters/e-mails home while aboard the space shuttle.
- Bring in freeze-dried "astronaut" food for the kids. (You can find a variety of freeze-dried foods wherever camping equipment is sold.)
- Have students tape record their imaginary trip.
- Play the audio of Neil Armstrong taking his "giant leap for mankind."
- Take students outside and let them move in slow motion to pretend they are moving or jumping in space.

Space Traveler's ID

Photo

Name: _____

_____

Home Planet: _____

_____

Space Traveler's ID

Photo

Name: _____

_____

Home Planet: _____

_____

Space Traveler's ID

Photo

Name: _____

_____

Home Planet: _____

_____

Space Traveler's ID

Photo

Name: _____

_____

Home Planet: _____

_____

Space Journal Page

Date:

Dear Journal,

Blast-Off!
Earth from Space

Benchmarks/Standards covered:
- Generate writing ideas through discussion with others.
- Use books or observations to gather information.
- Use nouns, verbs, and adjectives.

Books to explore:

It Looked Like Spilt Milk by Charles G. Shaw (HarperTrophy, 1988)
Earth: Our Planet in Space by Seymour Simon (Simon & Schuster, 2003)
The Moon Book by Gail Gibbons (Holiday House, 1998)

Discussion:

Many astronauts say one of the best things about their job is getting to see Earth from space. Some astronauts say Earth looks like a big, blue marble. American astronaut Dr. Kathryn Sullivan said she thought it looked like a blue, beach ball! Why do you think astronauts call the Earth a blue marble or a beach ball? (If not noted by students, point out the Earth is round and covered in water.)

Sometimes, writers describe one thing by comparing it to something else. This is called a simile. (Write the following on the board: Earth is as round as a big, blue marble. From space, Earth looks like a blue, beach ball. Underline the words as and like.) A simile uses the words *like* or *as*. For example, a writer might say "The other night, the moon looked like a pumpkin." Or "The girl was as pretty as a flower." What two things are being compared in these sentences? (Reread examples if necessary.) How can the moon look like a pumpkin? (Responses might include: it's round, it has a face, sometimes it's orange.) How can a girl be like a flower? (Responses might include: both are pretty, both smell good, both are small.)

Now it's your turn:

Last time we met, we blasted-off into space. Today, we're going to use our imaginations to write a description of Earth. Pretend you are floating out in space, riding in a space shuttle, and looking out the window down at Earth. Write a simile to describe our planet. (Hand out Earth worksheet or write the following on the board: *From space, Earth looks like a _____. From space, Earth is as _____ as a _____.*) Choose one of these sentences and fill it in. If you want, you can fill in both!

Reminders for student writers:

- If you're having trouble, brainstorm all the things you can think of that are round or blue or bright. Maybe something on your list will remind you of Earth.

- When you're finished writing your simile, draw a picture of Earth the way you imagine it looks from outer space.

Teaching tips:

- If available, display a photo of Earth that was taken from space.

- Encourage students to write a simile that describes what Mars or one of the other planets looks like from space.

- Bring in a telescope or encourage students to use one at home to look at the moon or stars at night.

Earth

From space, Earth looks like a _____.

From space, Earth is as _____

as a _____.

Blast-Off!
Good News/Bad News

Benchmarks/Standards covered:
- Deliver informational presentations that express an opinion.
- Generate ideas for written compositions.

Books to explore:

Magic School Bus Lost in the Solar System by Joanna Cole (Scholastic, 1992)

Floating in Space (Let's-Read-And-Find-Out Science 2) by Franklyn M. Brahley (HarperTrophy, 1998)

The Best Book of Spaceships by Ian Graham (Kingfisher, 1998)

Discussion:

Here's a question for everyone. How many people would like to travel in space? How many people would *not* like to travel in space? For those of you who would like to travel in space, can you tell me why? (Record a few of the answers which might include: get to go on an adventure, get to see other planets or stars or the moon up close, get to be famous, parents aren't there to boss you around.) For those of you who wouldn't like to travel in space, can you tell me why? (Record a few of the answers, which might include: the trip would take a long time, have to eat food from a tube or freeze-dried food all the time, it's dark in space, might miss my family and friends.) Looking at our answers, we can see that some things about space travel would be good news and other things would be bad news.

When there are some good things and some bad things about a situation, that's called conflict. All stories have some kind of conflict. If nothing ever happened in a story or the characters never had any problems to solve, it would be pretty boring!

Now it's your turn:

Now, you're going to have the opportunity to create some good news/bad news of your own. Think back to the question I asked before about traveling in space. Whether or not you would like to travel in space, try to brainstorm five good things about it and five not-so-good things about it.

One easy way to come up with a conflict is to think of a good thing and then think how it could also be bad. For example, you might write: "The good news is there'd be no parents around to boss me. The bad news is I'd miss my parents!" Or you could write: "The good news is I wouldn't have a bed to make in the morning. The bad news is I'd probably miss my pillow."

Reminders for student writers:

- If you get stuck, take a look at the list we made as a class for ideas.

- Another thing you can try if you're stuck is to imagine a trip you've taken in a car or airplane or bus. Did you get carsick? Might you get "shuttle sick?"

- Get creative! What would you miss about being on Earth? What might you experience riding in a space shuttle? Would it be cold? Cramped? Exciting? Like playing a giant video game?

Teaching tips:

- Pick one of the "bad news" items from the students' list and write a class story using that conflict.

- Expand on the good news/bad news theme by having students write a list of pros and cons about being their age.

- Find the conflicts in familiar stories. Talk about how these conflicts could be settled. For example, maybe Goldilocks could make more porridge or fix the chair she broke.

Blast-Off!
Ode to the Moon

Benchmarks/Standards covered:
- Use descriptive words and phrases.
- Deliver simple dramatic presentations.
- Explain how an author's word choice and use of methods influence the reader.

Books to explore:

The Moon Book by Gail Gibbons (Holiday House, 1998)

W*hat is the Moon Like?* by Franklin M. Branley (HarperTrophy, 2000)

Owl Moon by Jane Yolen (Philomel Books, 1987)

The Thirteen Moons on Turtle's Back: A Native American Year of Moons by Joseph Bruchac and Jonathan London (Putnam Publishing Group, 1997)

Discussion:

Today, I have a poem to share. (Put up Ode to The Sun transparency and read with plenty of expression.) What did you think of the poem? How about the way I read it? How did my voice sound? (Responses might include: happy, excited, silly.) This is a special kind of poem called an ode. An ode is a poem in which the poet pays tribute or praises something. How can we tell the poet likes the sun? (Responses might include: the poet uses the word "wonderful" and "favorite," talks about all the good things the sun does, uses many exclamation points.) Did we learn anything about the sun?

Let's try writing an ode together. What should we write about? What good things can we say about what we've chosen? What exciting words can we use in our ode to show how we feel? (After the class has written its ode, read the poem aloud together, encouraging students to use lots of expression.)

Now it's your turn:

Now, it's your turn to write an ode on your own. Instead of writing about the sun, we're going to write about something in space—the moon! The first thing you should do is brainstorm all the good things you can think about the moon. You can use the back of the worksheet or use another piece of paper. Next, write your ode using some of those ideas.

Reminders for student writers:

- Pretend you are describing the moon to someone who has never seen it or knows nothing about it. What would you tell that person if he or she asked why the moon was important or how it looked?

- Sometimes the moon looks orange or is out during the day. Can you think of anything else that's special or surprising about the moon?

- When you're finished, read your ode to a neighbor. Remember to use lots of expression!

Teaching tips:

- Bring in a model of the solar system or a picture of the moon.

- Create a class bulletin board with a giant moon and the students' odes around it or hang a paper moon from the ceiling and hang the odes around the room as well.

- There's a famous photo of the American flag planted on the moon. Invite students to create their own, personal flags to "plant" on the moon.

Ode to the Sun

Oh, Sun,

you are the biggest and best star around!

You help flowers grow

and make the sand at the beach warm.

You wake us up in the morning

and visit the other side of the world

when it's nighttime.

You are wonderful! Magnificent! Awesome!

What on Earth would we do without you?

Blast-Off!
Constellation Creations

Benchmarks/Standards covered:
- Construct complete sentences.
- Name or label objects.
- Use visual aids as sources to gain additional information.
- Tell simple stories using words or pictures.

Books to explore:

Find the Constellations by H.A. Rey (Houghton Mifflin, 1976)

Glow-in-the-Dark Constellations: A Field Guide for Young Stargazers by C.E. Thompson (Grosset and Dunlap, 1999)

Zoo in the Sky by Jacqueline Mitton (National Geographic Children's Books, 1998)

Coyote Places the Stars by Harriet Peck Taylor (Simon & Schuster, 1993)

How the Stars Fell into the Sky by Jerrie Oughton (Houghton Mifflin, 1996)

Discussion:

Have you ever looked at the stars at night? Sometimes, the night sky reminds me of a connect-the-dots picture. How about you? For thousands of years, people have looked at the stars and seen imaginary pictures. These imaginary pictures, made by a group of stars, are called constellations. There are 88 recognized constellations in our solar system. Some of them are more famous than others. Does anyone know the name of a constellation? (Responses might include: Leo, Aries, Orion, Gemini.) Has anyone ever pointed out the Big Dipper or the Little Dipper to you? The Big Dipper is part of a constellation called Ursa Major. The Little Dipper is part of Ursa Minor.

In addition to having names, the constellations have interesting stories. For example, have you ever heard of Orion's belt? (Put up transparency of Orion constellation. Point out Orion's belt and his shield.) Orion is the name of a great hunter from Greek mythology. According to the legend, he was a very handsome and skilled hunter who died when he stepped on Scorpius, a scorpion. It is said that after he died, Diana, an admirer of Orion, begged the gods to put him in the night sky so she could always remember him.

Now it's your turn:

How would you like to create your own constellation? (Hand out paper and star stickers.) First, design a constellation with your star stickers. If you want, you can sketch it out first on a piece of scrap paper or lightly sketch it out in pencil on your construction paper. Next, give your constellation a name and write a few sentences about what or who it's named after. (Students can then tape or glue their stories to the paper for display.)

Reminders for student writers:

- Don't forget to give your constellation a name. You can name it after yourself if you'd like!
- Your constellation doesn't have to look exactly like what it is. Remember, people who view your constellation can use their imaginations just like we did with Orion.

Teaching tips:

- Make a bulletin board with a night sky with and students' constellations.
- Ask students why they think people started to name constellations and give them stories. (Some experts believe constellations began as a way to remember stars and their positions.)
- If possible, visit a planetarium.
- Explore more Greek mythology or the legends behind the constellations.
- Take a look at this Web page for more constellation activities. <http://sciencespot.net/Pages/classastro.html>

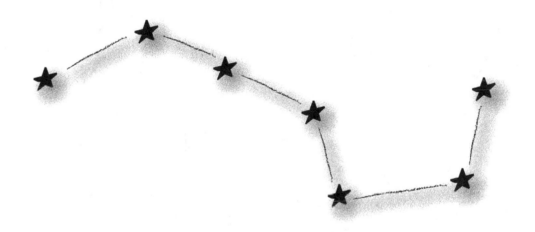

Orion

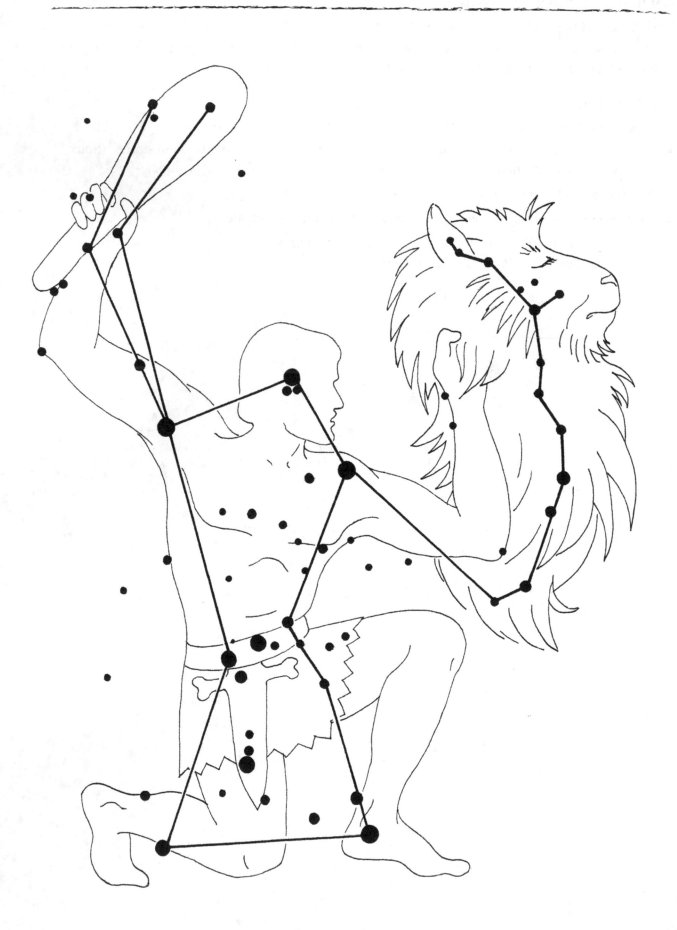

Workshop Overview:
Food Fun!

Everyone has a favorite (or least favorite) food and everyone eats! This is what makes these lessons so engaging. Though the title of the workshop suggests it, students will not be actually eating during this workshop. (Though, it's very easy and lots of fun to bring in various foods for the "Yuck" lesson.) In this workshop, students continue to use adjectives and descriptive phrases and understand how authors make choices to affect their readers. In addition, students will learn about various types of writing, such as reviews, poetry, and recipes. Students also get to practice recognizing beginning sounds as they create their own tongue twisters using their names.

To stir up some fun, students are given paper spoons at the beginning of this workshop.

Writing activities	Materials and handouts *(one copy for each student)*
My Favorite Food Tradition	Spoon made of tag board My Favorite Food transparency My Favorite Food worksheet Paper plates (optional)
Tongue Twisters	Tongue Twister transparency Write-it-then-draw-it paper (optional)
Yuck!	A Review of Sauerkraut transparency writing paper
A Recipe for Fun	A Good Soccer Game transparency Blank recipe cards (optional)
Scrambled Poem	Scrambled Poem worksheet

Food Fun!
My Favorite Food Tradition

Benchmarks/Standards covered:

- Connect prior experience, insights, and ideas to those of a speaker.
- Identify words from text that appeal to senses.
- Deliver brief, descriptive presentations recalling an event or personal experience that convey relevant information and descriptive details.
- Use resources to select effective vocabulary.

Books to explore:

Cloudy with a Chance of Meatballs by Judi Barrett (Aladdin, 1982) and its sequel, *Pickles to Pittsburgh* (Aladdin, 2000)
How My Parents Learned to Eat by Ina R. Friedman (Houghton Mifflin, 1987)
The Giant Jam Sandwich by John Vernon Lord and Janet Burroway (Houghton Mifflin, 1975)

Discussion:

I'd like to tell you about a fun, food tradition we have in my family. (Share a food tradition such as: always having tamales on Christmas Eve, getting to choose your favorite meal on your birthday, eating breakfast for dinner on Friday nights.) Traditions are things we do over and over, usually as part of a celebration. They can be a lot of fun because they help us look forward to a special time and then help make that special time even better. How many of you have some kind of food tradition at home? Great! Today, we're going to get a chance to "stir up" some fun by writing about our favorite food traditions. Here is an example of what you'll get the chance to do in a few moments. (Put up My Favorite Food transparency and read together.) What senses does the writer use to describe the pumpkin seeds? (Sight, smell, taste.)

Now it's your turn:

Take a few minutes and think about all your favorite food traditions. (Pass out My Favorite Food worksheet.) When you're ready, begin filling in the blanks. Take your time! If it helps, close your eyes and imagine yourself eating that favorite food. What does it look like? What does it smell like? Does it make a sound when you bite it? What tradition is this food connected to? Has your family always eaten this food or is this something new? Draw a picture of your favorite food.

Reminders for student writers:

- In our example, the writer used the word mmmarvelous to describe pumpkin seeds. Challenge yourself to find fun descriptive words to describe your favorite food. Use a dictionary or thesaurus to help.
- When you're finished, you can decorate your spoon. (Have tag board spoons available if they have not been passed out already.)

Teaching tips:

- Have students cut out their answers and glue them on a paper plate as a fun way to display their work!

- Make a class graph of favorite foods.

- Have a Favorite Food Day when students bring in samples of their favorite foods to share.

- Discuss other family traditions students may have or start some kind of class tradition.

Spoon Template

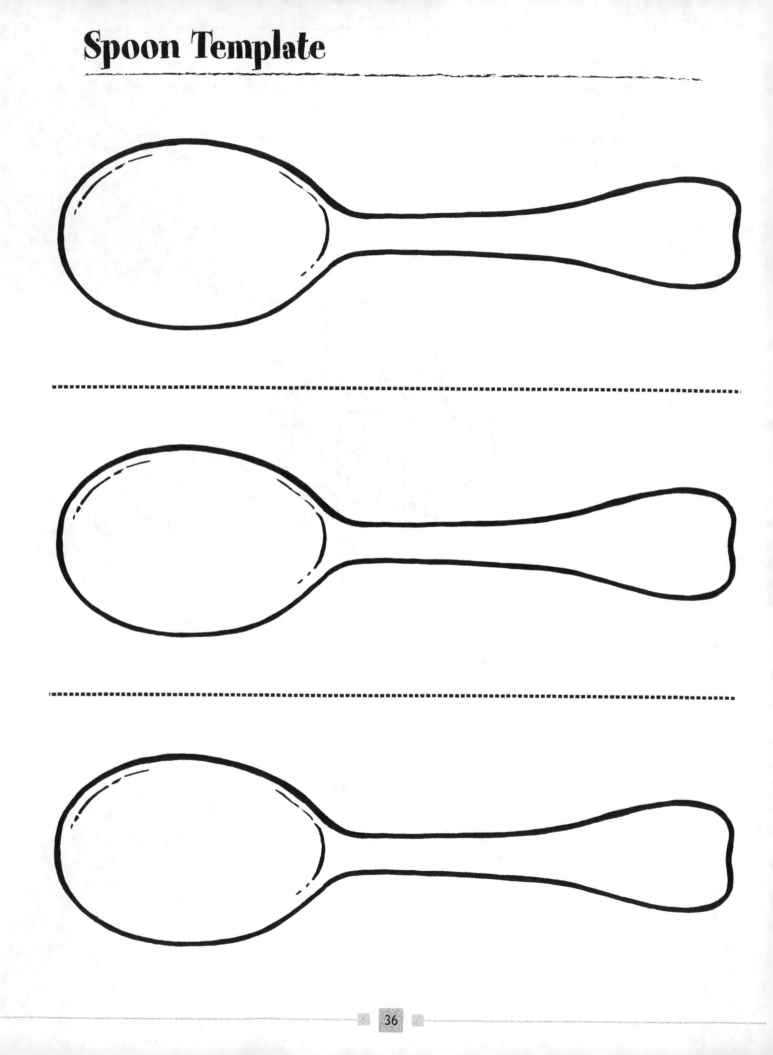

My Favorite Food

My favorite food is **pumpkin seeds.**

Its color is **white.**

It smells **buttery.**

It's best eaten when **it's right out of the oven.**

It's best eaten with **cold milk.**

Our family tradition: **We roast pumpkin seeds every Halloween. We do it right after we carve the jack-o-lantern.**

The one word that best describes my favorite food:

Mmmarvelous!

37

My Favorite Food

This is a picture of me eating my favorite food.

My favorite food is _____.

Its color is _____.

It smells _____.

It's best eaten when_____.

It's best eaten with_____.

Our family tradition_____

_____

_____.

The one word that best describes my favorite food:

_____.

Food Fun!
Tongue Twisters

Benchmarks/Standards covered:
- Distinguish and identify the beginning sounds in words.
- Use nouns, verbs, and adjectives.
- Reread own writing.

Books to explore:

Six Sick Sheep: One Hundred Tongue Twisters by Joanna Cole and Stephanie Calmeson (HarperTrophy, 1993)

Giggle Fit: Zany Tongue Twisters by Joseph Rosenbloom and Mike Artell (Sterling, 2003)

Alligator Arrived with Apples: A Potluck Alphabet Feast by Crescent Dragonwagon (Aladdin, 1992)

Creepy Crawly Critters and other Halloween Tongue Twisters by Nola Buck (HarperTrophy, 1996)

Discussion:

What do you notice about these sentences? (Put up Tongue Twisters transparency. If not noted by students, point out that they repeat a letter sound throughout.) Let's read them aloud. These are fun but kind of challenging to say out loud, aren't they? They are called tongue twisters. Does anyone know any other tongue twisters? (Take a few minutes to allow students to share.) Tongue twisters often use a special writer's trick called alliteration. Alliteration is using the same beginning letter sound throughout a sentence. (Read through each sentence again and ask students to identify the beginning letter sound being repeated.) Let's take one more look at the last two sentences. Notice anything different about them? (If not noted, point out that the beginning *sounds* are the same, not just the *beginning* letters; the letter "G" is soft and the letter "C" is hard.)

Now it's your turn:

Think about your own name. What beginning sound does it have? See if you can write a tongue twister using your name. Don't worry if you can't think of enough words; each word in your tongue twister doesn't have to have the same sound. (Point out that several of the examples use words with different beginning sounds.) Try to think of things you can do or like to do. Get silly! Have fun! When you're finished, read your tongue twister out loud.

Reminders for student writers:

- If you get stuck and can't think of a good word, ask a neighbor if he or she has any ideas. You can also look up a letter in the dictionary.

- See how many tongue twisters you can come up with using your name. Can you think of three? Four? More?

- When you're finished, illustrate your tongue twister.

- Try coming up with a tongue twister with some one else's name, like a friend or your mom or dad or sibling.

Teaching tips:

- Create a class book with all the name tongue twisters.

- Display the tongue twisters on a bulletin board outside of the classroom so other students in school can enjoy and try them.

- Let students tape record themselves trying to say the tongue twisters.

Tongue Twisters

Lisa likes to lick lemony lollipops.

On Monday, maybe Michael and Molly will make their mom macaroni.

Isabel isn't eating icky ice cream.

Josh just doesn't jump off jungle gyms.

Kaitlin carefully counts carrot cakes for the carnival cake walk.

Food Fun!
Yuck!

Benchmarks/Standards covered:
- Use descriptive words and phrases.
- Explain how the author's word choice and use of methods influence the reader.
- Use various tools to enhance vocabulary.
- Recognize the defining characteristics and features of different types of literary forms and genres.

Books to explore:

Stink Soup! by Jill Esbaum (Farrar, Straus & Giroux, 2004)
Poem Stew by William Cole (HarperTrophy, 1983)
How to Eat Fried Worms by Thomas Rockwell (Yearling, 1953)
Freckle Juice by Judy Blume (Yearling, 1978)
Roald Dahl's Revolting Recipes by Roald Dahl (Puffin, 1997)

Discussion:

I bet you all have a favorite food. But does anyone have a *least* favorite food? A food you tried once and hated, or a food you would never in a million years be willing to try? (Put up A Review of Sauerkraut transparency.) This is a review about sauerkraut. A review is piece of writing in which someone talks about what they like or don't like or what they think about a particular thing. Reviews can be about all kinds of things. Can you think of anything people write reviews about? (Responses might include books, movies, television shows, plays, concerts, restaurants. Read the example aloud for students.) How does Sara feel about sauerkraut? We know she doesn't just dislike sauerkraut; she hates it! And we know this because she uses strong words. What strong words or phrases does Sara use? (Responses might include: made me try it, yuck, slimy, sour, bitter taste, made my whole body shiver in disgust, you'd be crazy to swallow one, tiny piece.) Did you notice how Sara used all five of her senses to describe sauerkraut? (Go back and point out each example.) Sara also used a good variety of adjectives, or describing words.

Now it's your turn:

Today, you get a chance to get even with your least favorite food by writing an unfavorable review. Think of the one food you absolutely, positively can't stand and then write a paragraph telling us why. Tell us about the first time you tried it, or if you've never tried it, why you avoid it. What's so terrible about this particular food? Does it make you gag? Throw up? Want to run from the room, holding your nose? If you have strong feelings, use strong words. Reviews often give readers advice about what to try or not try, too. Do you have any advice about eating this food? Look back at the example: Sara says, "Never try sauerkraut!"

Reminders for student writers:

- Remember to describe the food using all of your senses. What does the food smell, taste, feel, sound, look like?

- Brainstorm a list of adjectives about the food you've chosen. Add a few of them to your review.

Teaching tips:

- Read *Green Eggs and Ham* by Dr. Seuss and have students share a time when they thought they wouldn't like a certain food, tried it, and discovered they did. Celebrate trying something new by having a Green Eggs and Ham Day. Serve real green eggs and ham.

- Discuss strange or unusual foods people in other countries eat or consider a delicacy.

- Create a fun bulletin board by putting up the reviews and picket signs that announce students are "on strike" from eating these foods.

- Have students write reviews about other things such as books they've read or movies they've seen.

A Review of Sauerkraut
By Sara, age 10

Sauerkraut is the most disgusting thing in the world. My dad made me try it a couple of weeks ago. When he put it into the pan, it made a splat! It smelled like raw fish. Yuck! He plopped it onto my plate, and it looked like something that had already been chewed and spit out in slimy, stringy shreds. (If you've ever put a worm in your mouth, you know what it feels like to have sauerkraut in your mouth.) The sour, bitter taste was the worst part of all. It made my whole body shiver in disgust. Never try sauerkraut! You'd have to be crazy to swallow one, tiny piece.

Food Fun!
A Recipe for Fun

Benchmarks/Standards covered:

- Use nouns, verbs, and adjectives.
- Compose writings that convey a clear message and include well-chosen details.
- Use revision strategies and resources to improve ideas and content, organization, word choice, and detail.

Books to explore:

Dim Sum for Everyone by Grace Lin (Knopf Books for Young Readers, 2001)
The Tortilla Factory by Gary Paulsen (Voyager Books, 1998)
Dumpling Soup by Jama Kim Rattigan (Megan Tingley, 1998)
Three Days on a River in a Red Canoe by Vera B. Williams (HarperTrophy, 1984)

Discussion:

If I wanted to make some cupcakes and didn't know what to do, what could I use to help me? Right! I could use a cookbook! Cookbooks have recipes. Has anyone seen a recipe? What kind of information is in a recipe? (Responses might include: the name of the dish, the ingredients, directions for cooking, how to tell when a dish is ready.) Most recipes you've seen have probably been for food. Recipes can be for other things, though, too. Here's one. (Handout copies of How to Make a Good Soccer Game Recipe and read aloud.) What do you think of this recipe? Does it give you all the information you need? (Invite students to add any "ingredient" they feel is missing.) Did you notice how the recipe has three parts: the title, the list of ingredients, and the directions? Let's try writing another recipe together. What would a recipe for A Good Classroom look like? (As a group, write recipe.)

Now it's your turn:

Think of something you really enjoy and write a recipe for it. It can be anything at all! For example, a game you like to play, the perfect Saturday, a good vacation, a special celebration. First, you'll need a title so readers will know what kind of fun you're cooking up. Next, you should make a list of all the things, or ingredients, that go into making that fun activity. And finally, give some directions on how to mix the ingredients or complete the recipe. For example, do you need a certain amount of time to do the activity? Do you have to do it in a certain place or at a certain time of year?

Reminders for student writers:

- Challenge yourself to find fun action words like sprinkle, toss in, or simmer.
- When you're done, trade your work with a neighbor. Read your neighbor's recipe and see if he or she missed anything. Ask him or her if you missed any important ingredients or instructions.

Teaching tips:

- Bring in old recipes but cut off or hide the name of the dish. Let students guess what the recipe is for.

- Let students write their recipes on real recipe cards.

- Collect the students' recipes and create a class book called "Recipes for Fun."

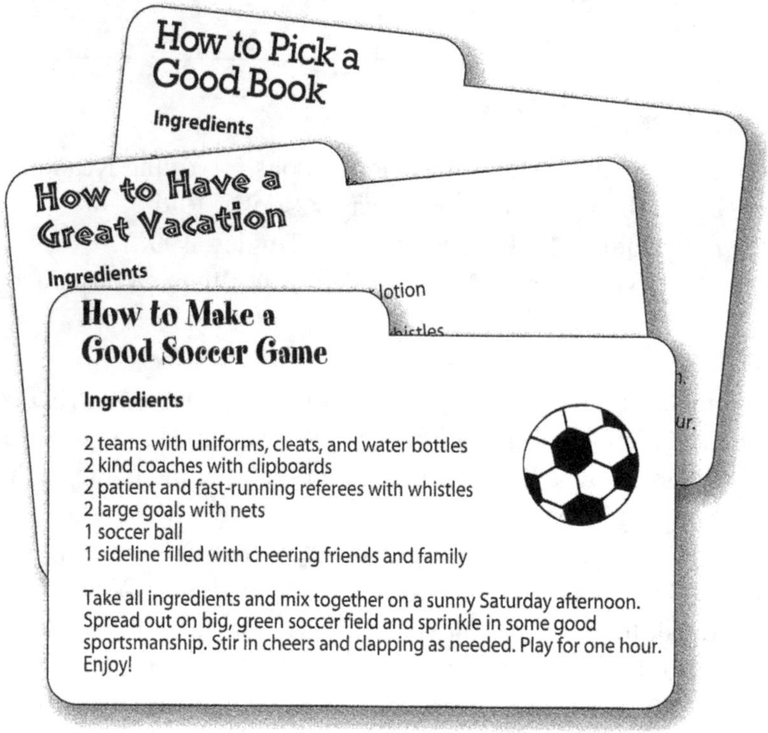

How to Pick a
Good Book

Ingredients

How to Have a
Great Vacation

Ingredients

...lotion

...histles

...ur.

How to Make a
Good Soccer Game

Ingredients

2 teams with uniforms, cleats, and water bottles
2 kind coaches with clipboards
2 patient and fast-running referees with whistles
2 large goals with nets
1 soccer ball
1 sideline filled with cheering friends and family

Take all ingredients and mix together on a sunny Saturday afternoon. Spread out on big, green soccer field and sprinkle in some good sportsmanship. Stir in cheers and clapping as needed. Play for one hour. Enjoy!

How to Make a Good Soccer Game Recipe

How to Make a Good Soccer Game

Ingredients

2 teams with uniforms, cleats, and water bottles
2 kind coaches with clipboards
2 patient and fast-running referees with whistles
2 large goals with nets
1 soccer ball
1 sideline filled with cheering friends and family

Take all ingredients and mix together on a sunny Saturday afternoon. Spread out on big, green soccer field and sprinkle in some good sportsmanship. Stir in cheers and clapping as needed. Play for one hour. Enjoy!

How to Make a Good Soccer Game

Ingredients

2 teams with uniforms, cleats, and water bottles
2 kind coaches with clipboards
2 patient and fast-running referees with whistles
2 large goals with nets
1 soccer ball
1 sideline filled with cheering friends and family

Take all ingredients and mix together on a sunny Saturday afternoon. Spread out on big, green soccer field and sprinkle in some good sportsmanship. Stir in cheers and clapping as needed. Play for one hour. Enjoy!

Food Fun!
Scrambled Poem

Benchmarks/Standards covered:
- Produce informal writings.
- Use various tools and resources to enhance vocabulary.
- Use organizers to clarify ideas for writing assignments.

Books to explore:

The Scrambled States of America by Laurie Keller (Henry Holt and Co., 2002)
Chicka Chicka Boom Boom by Bill Martin Jr. (Aladdin, 2000)
Scrambled Eggs Supper by Dr. Seuss (Random House, 1953)

Discussion:

When you'd like to write a poem, sometimes the best plan of action is to pick a subject and start brainstorming, or make a list of all the words you could think of that go with it. For example, if I wrote the word school, what words could you think of that go along with it? (Record a good sample of the responses.) Wow! We sure have a lot of good ideas all scrambled together. Let's see if we can unscramble our ideas and use some of the words to write a poem about school. (Rearrange some of the words and add words as needed to create a brief poem about school and read together.) The poem we wrote is a special kind of poem. It's called a list poem. Can anyone guess why? (Responses might include: you make a list first, you use words from a list, the poem sounds like a list.) Let's make another list. Since our workshop is called Food Fun, let's brainstorm words that have to do with food—eating food, smelling food, tasting—anything! (Record answers on board.)

Now it's your turn:

Our food words list looks great. Now, it's time to make our own scrambled poems! (Pass out Scrambled Poem worksheet.) I'm passing out a worksheet with some food and eating words already on it. See if any of the words we came up with are there! As you can see, only some of the sheet is filled out. I'd like for you to fill in the rest of the squares on your own. You can use some of the words we have up on the board, if you'd like, or come up with new ones.

After you've filled all the squares, carefully cut them out. Next, comes the really fun part! Mix the words all around, scramble them up all different ways, and see if you can cook up a food poem you like. When you get one, write it down on a blank piece of paper.

Reminders for student writers:

- Remember your five senses when you're coming up with words. Throw in a few words that have to do with color, smell, taste, sound, and touch.

- You can add words here and there to help your poem make sense.

- Don't worry if you can't come up with a poem right away, and don't think you have to write down the very first one you come up with. Just have fun playing around, rearranging the words.

Teaching tips:

- Have a Scrambled Poetry Party where students can read their work. Invite parents and grandparents and serve scrambled eggs.

- Bring in Magnetic Poetry™ sets and let students explore or make your own version using note cards. Add small strips of magnetic strip to each card and use an old cookie sheet or other magnetic surface.

Scrambled Poem

Directions: Pick a topic and make a list of all the words that go along with it. Write the words in the spaces below. When you're ready, cut the words out and move them around to create a poem. Add words to your poem if you need to in order for it to make sense.

sizzle		
		delicious
	aroma	
mix		
	slurp	
Mmmm!		tasty

Workshop Overview:
Let's Go!

Students are on the move in this workshop. They're learning about making checklists (an early form of outlines) and putting ideas into categories as they "sleep over at a friend's house." In "If I Were the Principal," they get to pretend to be in charge and use their growing persuasive writing skills to change a school rule. In "My Favorite Place" and "Scary Story," students will also explore the concept of setting, an important story element.

To encourage students to let their imaginations travel around, I like to give them their own fake driver's license. If possible, let students add their class photos for an extra fun and authentic touch.

Writing activities	Materials and handouts (one copy for each student)
Sleep Over	Creative License My Sleep Over Checklist worksheet
If I Were the Principal	New Principal worksheet
Just Down the Road	Writing paper
My Favorite Place	Large construction paper, folded in half width-wise
Scary Story	The Old Man in the Shack transparency

Lets Go!
Sleep Over

Benchmarks/Standards covered:
- Deliver brief informal descriptive presentations recalling an event or personal experience that convey relevant information and descriptive details.
- Organize and group related ideas.
- Follow multi-step oral directions.

Books to explore:

Ira Sleeps Over by Bernard Waber (Houghton Mifflin, 1975)
Little Critter Sleeps Over by Mercer Mayer (Random House Books for Young Readers, 1999)
Ten Minutes Till Bedtime by Peggy Rathman (G.P. Putnam's Sons, 2001)
How Do Dinosaurs Say Goodnight? by Jane Yolen (Blue Sky Press, 2000)

Discussion:

Have you ever spent the night at someone else's house? Sleeping over can be a lot of fun. What are some of the special things you've done on a sleep over? (Invite students to share a little bit about their experiences.) One of the best parts of going on a sleep over is getting ready. It's fun to plan! Sometimes people plan by first making a list of things they don't want to forget. Lists can be very helpful. For example, if we were going on a field trip to a farm, what would we want to be sure to bring with us? (Responses might include: warm clothes, boots, a sack lunch.) We might also want to make a list of things we would want to do. How would having these lists be helpful? (Responses might include: so we don't forget anything, so we set priorities. If applicable, point out any lists you have in the class.)

Now it's your turn:

Today, we're going to pretend we've been invited to our friends' houses to sleep over. Now, the big night is still a few days away. We have plenty of time to get ready and plan. One of the things we want to do is make some lists. (Hand out My Sleep Over Checklist worksheet.) The first list I want you to make is all the things you want to take with you on your sleep over. They can be things you need like a toothbrush or a pillow, and things you just want to take, like a stuffed animal or a board game. The second list I want you to make is the activities you want to do on your sleep over. These activities might be a game to play, or a movie to watch or a favorite food to eat or a craft to make.

Reminders for student writers:

- Think about what you'll need in the morning, too.
- Pretend you can take only one bag. Is there anything on your list your friend might already have and could share?

Teaching tips:

- Challenge older students to make a step-by-step list of what they do to get ready for bed. For example: (1) Brush teeth (2) Get pajamas (3) Read bedtime story.

- Have a pretend sleep over in the classroom in which students bring sleeping bags, make s'mores, and tell ghost stories.

- Have students make a list of things they'd need if they were spending a *week* at a friend's house.

- Make a class graph about the students' favorite bedtime snacks.

Creative License

Creative License

Name:
Age:
School:

The bearer of this card is hearby licensed to get creative and let his or her imagination travel to new and exciting places!

Creative License

Name:
Age:
School:

The bearer of this card is hearby licensed to get creative and let his or her imagination travel to new and exciting places!

Creative License

Name:
Age:
School:

The bearer of this card is hearby licensed to get creative and let his or her imagination travel to new and exciting places!

Creative License

Name:
Age:
School:

The bearer of this card is hearby licensed to get creative and let his or her imagination travel to new and exciting places!

Creative License

Name:
Age:
School:

The bearer of this card is hearby licensed to get creative and let his or her imagination travel to new and exciting places!

Creative License

Name:
Age:
School:

The bearer of this card is hearby licensed to get creative and let his or her imagination travel to new and exciting places!

✔ My Sleep Over Checklist

These are things I want to take:

_____

_____

_____

_____

_____

These are the things I want to do:

_____

_____

_____

_____

_____

My Sleep Over Checklist

Let's Go!
If I Were the Principal

Benchmarks/Standards covered:
- Use personal pronouns.
- Dictate or write informal writings.
- Determine purpose and audience in writing.

Books to explore:

Duck for President by Doreen Cronin (Simon & Schuster, 2004)
The Principal from the Black Lagoon by Mike Thaler (Scholastic, 1993)
The Frog Principal by Stephanie Calmeson (Scholastic, 2001)
A Fine, Fine School by Sharon Creech (Joanna Colter, 2001)
It's Back to School We Go by Ellen Jackson (Millbrook Press, 2003)

Discussion:

Have you ever wondered what it would be like to be in charge? Do you think being in charge of a school would be fun? What might be challenging about being in charge? (Ask children to further explain their responses.) One of the many jobs a principal has is to help make the rules. (If time permits, discuss why rules are important.) What are some of the rules we have here at school? Are there any rules you would change if you were in charge? Why would you change that rule? Are there any other changes about the school day you'd make if you were the principal? (Record as many of the responses as you can on the board so students can refer to them later on.) For example, would you make recess longer? Serve pizza for lunch every day? Allow kids to wear pajamas on Fridays?

Now it's your turn:

Pretend you have just been named the new principal at our school. As your first order of business, you must give a short announcement about a new rule you've made or a change you've made. (Hand out New Principal worksheet.) Think about what you would definitely like to change if you were suddenly in charge of the school. Sorry! Closing school for good isn't an option! After you've decided on your new rule, explain to the other students and teachers why you made it. For example, let's say you decide that pizza should be served every day at lunch. What might be the benefits of having pizza everyday? (Responses might include: most people like it, you don't need a fork to eat it, the school could order it from a pizza place, which means the cafeteria workers would have less work.) When you're ready, fill in the blanks on the worksheet.

Reminders for student writers:

- If you're stuck for an idea, check the board. Maybe one of those ideas will get you started.
- Have fun making up a new rule or changing an old one, but remember to be respectful. Your new rule or change cannot hurt or embarrass anyone.
- Try to come up with at least one reason you're making the change. If you can think of more than one reason, great! Include them in your announcement, too.

Teaching tips:

- Have students write letters to the principal, stating what one change they'd like to see and why.

- If your principal is willing, let students be "Principal for a Day" (or afternoon or hour) so that they can see what goes on behind the scenes in the office. Have them make predictions about what it's like to be a principal; afterwards, ask them if their predictions were accurate.

- Extend the project into the home by having students write an essay called "If I Were the Parent."

- Make a "Top Ten Things We'd Change" list for a hallway bulletin board.

New Principal Worksheet

"Good morning, Students and Teachers! I'm Principal
_____

I'd like to announce that beginning today
_____
_____
_____ .

I've decided to make this change because
_____
_____
_____
_____ ."

Principal for the day

"Good morning, Students and Teachers! I'm Principal
_____

I'd like to announce that beginning today
_____
_____
_____ .

I've decided to make this change because
_____
_____
_____
_____ ."

Principal for the day

Let's Go!
Just down the Road

Benchmarks/Standards covered:
- Identify words in common categories such as color words, number words, and directional words.
- Apply tools to judge the quality of writing.

Books to explore:

On the Town: A Community Adventure by Judith Casely (Greenwillow, 2002)
Over the River and Through the Woods by Lydia Marie Child (Henry Holt & Co., 1999)
Grandpa's Corner Store by DyAnne DiSalva-Ryan (HarperCollins, 2000)
Me on the Map by Joan Sweeney (Dragonfly Books, 1998)
Bears in the Night by Stan Berenstain (Random House, 1971)

Discussion:

How many of you walked backwards to our classroom this morning? No one? That would be silly, wouldn't it? You need to *see* where you're going to get there. Maps are one tool we can use when we need to know how to get somewhere. Can anyone think of another tool we might use? (Responses might include: online sites such as MapQuest™, verbal directions.) Written directions are another way we could make sure to get where we want to go. Who might we ask for directions? (Responses may include: friend, parent, neighbor, police officer, the receptionist at the place we're going.)

Let's pretend I'm a new student in our classroom and I need to know where the library is. Starting from the classroom door, what directions would you give me? (Write the students' directions on the board, numbering the steps.) What are some of the good direction words we used? Let's circle them. (Circle words such as left, right, up, north, west, go past, etc.) Landmarks are things or places that are easily seen and help us when we are using verbal or written directions. For instance, the blue tile star by the front doors (or appropriate example) is a good landmark because it's so big. Did we use any landmarks? (Underline any landmarks.)

Now it's your turn:

Pick a place you like to go. Starting at your home's front door, write directions to the place you chose. Make your directions as simple as possible. Include direction words like the ones we circled on the board. Number your steps like we did in our example. Whoever is using your directions doesn't have to walk; they can take a car or a bike if the place you picked is far away.

When you're done, have someone read your directions to you. Close your eyes and imagine the trip. Did you get where you wanted to go?

Reminders for student writers:

- Give your readers at least two landmarks to use.

- Don't forget to give your directions a title, such as "How to Get to the Park."

- If you'd like, draw a map to go along with your directions when you're finished.

Teaching tips:

- For a fun twist, have students close their eyes and give them directions to a place in the school. See if kids can determine where your imaginary trip took them.

- Take students on a neighborhood walk and have them write down or illustrate the landmarks they see.

- Have students make a map of the school or neighborhood.

- Act out *Bears in the Night*.

Let's Go!
My Favorite Place

Benchmarks/Standards covered:
- Use supporting details to identify and describe main ideas, characters, and settings.
- Use descriptive words and phrases.
- Illustrate own writing.

Books to explore:

A Quiet Place by Douglas Wood (Simon & Schuster, 2001)
All the Places to Love by Patricia MacLachlan (HarperCollins, 1994)
When I Was Young in the Mountains by Cynthia Rylant (Dutton Children's' Books, 1985)

Discussion:

Close your eyes and imagine you are standing in the middle of your favorite place in the whole world. In your head, answer these questions: Where are you? Are you inside or outside? What do you see? What do you hear? What do you smell or feel? Are you alone? If not, who's there with you? Try to collect as many details as you can. Open your eyes. Do you know what you just did? You created a setting! Writers create settings all the time. A setting is the place where a story or poem happens. If a writer has done his or her job well, a reader can almost "see" the place the story or poem describes.

Let's see what kind of job I can do describing a setting. (Describe the classroom or some other familiar place for students.) Where am I talking about? Did you notice how many adjectives, or describing words, I used? What were some of the details I included?

Now it's your turn:

On a piece of "sloppy copy paper," create a setting for your readers. Write about your favorite place or pick another place you think is interesting. Paint a picture of the place you want others to see by using as many details as you can. Tell us about what you see, what you hear, what you can feel or smell or taste. When you are happy with your paragraph, write the final version on the outside of the folded paper. (Hand out large pieces of construction paper that have been folded in half.) Next, open up the paper and draw a picture of the place you wrote about.

Reminders for student writers:

- You might want to begin with: The place I'm thinking of has …. Or: The place I'm thinking of is ….
- Try to think of a unique place, a place where no one else will think of.
- Include colors in your description.
- Before you start drawing, reread your description. Add those details to your illustration.

Teaching tips:

- As a group, describe the classroom setting.

- After reading a book in the classroom, see if students can identify the setting. Keep a running list of good story settings.

- Put setting/illustrations up on a bulletin board. Encourage students to read the settings and then open the flaps to see if they "saw" what the author did.

Let's Go!
Scary Story

Benchmarks/Standards covered:
- Explain how an author's word choice and use of methods influence the reader.
- Recognize the defining characteristics and features of different types of literary forms and genres.
- Identify the characters and setting in a story.
- Organize writing to include a beginning, middle, and end.

Books to explore:

The Little Old Lady Who Was Not Afraid of Anything by Linda Williams (HarperTrophy, 1988)
In a Dark, Dark Room and Other Scary Stories by Alvin Schwartz (HarperTrophy, 1985)
Boo! by Robert Munsch (Cartwheel Books, 2004)
A Very Hairy, Scary Story by Rick Walton (Grosset and Dunlap, 2004)
Who Took My Hairy Toe? By Shutta Crum (Albert Whitman & Co., 2001)

Discussion:

One of the best parts of camping is sitting around a campfire and telling scary stories. It's fun to be scared sometimes! A good, scary story can give you shivers or make you jump. It does this by building suspense. Suspense is the excited or anxious feeling you get when you feel something is about to happen. One way writers build suspense is by making sure their stories have good beginnings, middles and endings. Listen while I read this scary story out loud. (Put up The Old Man in the Shack transparency and read with plenty of expression.) What is the story's setting? (An old shack.) Tell me in one sentence, what happened in the beginning of the story. (The old man is alone in the shack and hears a noise.) What happened in the middle of the story? (The man finds out the sound is from someone who works for the electric company.) How did the story end? (The electric company man disappears.)

Another way authors build suspense is by using words that set a spooky or "I wonder what's going to happen next" mood. The author of our example used some words that helped set the mood for the story and let us know the main character was scared. Can you find any of them? (Responses may include: Spook Hill, pitch black, suddenly, scritch, trembling, slowly reached out. You may want to circle these words on the transparency.) What are some other words a writer might use in a scary story? (Record the students' responses on the board. Encourage students to include sound words such as: creak, bam, scratch, eeek.) What are some other good settings for a spooky story? (Record responses on board.)

Now it's your turn:

Choose one of the settings on the board. Next, write a scary story with a beginning, middle, and ending. Keep things simple by having only one, two, or three characters. Create a mood for your story by using scary words or sound words like the ones we wrote on the board.

It might help to make an outline before you begin. On a separate piece of paper, write the numbers one, two, and three. Beside each number, write one sentence about what happens first, second, and third.

Reminders for student writers:

- Try to paint a good picture of your setting with your words. Remember, you want your readers to be able to see the place you are describing in their minds.

- You may choose a setting that's not on the board if you like.

- Your ending doesn't have to be scary. It can funny or surprising. For example, maybe the "ghost" turned out to be a shadow or the main character was just having a bad dream.

Teaching tips:

- Turn off the classroom lights, gather together on the floor and share spooky stories. Serve s'mores. Set up a tape recorder and tape the students as they read.

- Create a class "Campfire Stories" book.

- Have students write the first paragraph of a scary story. Next, have them trade papers so they finish someone else's opening.

- During science class, create Monster Spray using spray bottles, water, and oils. Discuss how some smells, such as lavender, make us feel better or calmer.

The Old Man in the Shack

Once there was an old man who lived by himself in a shack. It was an old shack and in the middle of nowhere. It had peeling paint and a broken porch. And when the wind blew hard, the walls of the shack seemed to moan.

Late one night, the man was watching his favorite show, "Spook Hill." Suddenly, the electricity went out! It was pitch black.

The man was wondering what he should do when he heard a *scritch, scritch, scritch* on his front door. "Who…who's there?" the man called out nervously.

There was no answer, just *scritch, scritch, scritch.* And then…BAM! A loud knock!

Even though his legs were trembling, the man got up from his chair and made his way to the door. When he got there, he reached out his hand. The doorknob was ice cold. Slowly, he turned it. The old man took a deep breath, found his courage and flung the door open to face whoever—or whatever—was waiting for him!

"Sir?" a voice said. "Sir. I'm from the electric company. I've come to fix the lights."

The old man felt a little foolish for being afraid. He invited the worker inside and chatted with him while he worked.

In no time at all, the lights were back on. "Thanks," said the old man. "Can I make you some nice, hot coffee for your trip back into town?"

"That would be very nice," said the worker.

The old man turned around to make the coffee. But when he turned back to ask the worker if he wanted sugar in his coffee, the old man discovered that worker had—vanished into thin air!

Workshop Overview: Animals, Animals, Animals

Whether they're exotic animals in the zoo or furry creatures in our homes, animals are a great source of inspiration for writing. Most young children love animals and find this workshop a favorite. In the first activity, students learn about compound words (and how to let their imaginations go wild!) In the second activity, children continue to use their persuasive writing skills and begin to learn proper letter format as they try to convince their parents to get them a new pet. Students also learn about point of view and writing as a character, as well as how to conduct research for an informative writing activity.

The transitional item I like to use for this workshop is an animal mask that children can decorate. Masks can be worn by poking holes and adding strings on the side. You can also have children simply glue straws or craft sticks to their masks and let them hold them up to their faces.

Writing activities	Materials and handouts *(one copy for each student)*
Weird Animals	Animal Mask Blank, drawing paper
I Want a Pet	Writing paper
Who Am I Talking About?	Writing paper
Yours Truly	Writing paper
All About	Research Plan worksheet Various non-fiction books about animals (optional)

Animals, Animals, Animals
Weird Animals

Benchmarks/Standards covered:
- Predict the meaning of compound words using knowledge of individual words.
- Illustrate writing samples for display or sharing.

Books to explore:

If I Ran the Zoo by Dr. Seuss (Random House, 1950)
Wackiest White House Pets by Gibbs Davis (Scholastic Press, 2004)
Weird Friends: Unlikely Allies in the Animal Kingdom by Jose Aruego (Gulliver Books, 2002)
What Do You Do with a Tale Like That? by Robin Page, Steve Jenkins (Houghton Mifflin, 2003)
Platypus! by Ginger L. Clarke (Random House Books for Young Children, 2004)

Discussion:

A platypus is a strange looking animal. It is a small, furry animal that likes the water, has a tail like a beaver, and webbed feet and a bill like a duck! When people first reported seeing such a strange animal, scientists didn't believe them.

Let's see if we can create our own unbelievable animals. Someone name an animal. (Record several of the student's suggestions on the board.) Now that we have a few to choose from, let's pick two that would be fun to combine and circle them. If we put them together we get __. (Combine the two animals names into one word.) What we did here is kind of special. We made a new compound word. Compound words are two words that are put together to make a new one. Baseball, sunflower, and bedroom are all examples of compound words. Can you think of a few more? (Take just a few suggestions; save a longer lesson on compound words for later.)

Let's go back to our new, weird animal. What do you suppose (name of animal) would look like? (If you are artistic, sketch out a combination of the two animals. If not, invite two students to draw; one can do the top half and one can draw the bottom half.)

Now it's your turn:

Pretend you've been visiting in the deepest of jungles or the most remote lands. While you were there, you encountered a new and very strange animal. Now that you've returned home, the scientist who lives next door is bugging you to draw and name what you saw. (Pass out a piece of blank paper.) When you get a piece of paper, fold it in half.* Then, create a new animal by combining the upper half of one animal with the bottom half of another. Write the compound word name of the animal on the paper somewhere.

Reminders for student writers:

- Think about what kind of characteristics might be fun to combine. For example, if you want your animal to be fast, you could make its legs like a cheetah. If you want it to have long ears, you can make it look like a rabbit on top.

- When you're done outlining your new animal, begin coloring it in. Remember, this creature is your creation, so feel free to change colors or give it polka dots or some other unique look.

Teaching tips:

- *A variation: don't have students fold paper in half and allow them to combine animals any way they want. For example, they could put wings on an elephant body.

- Have students draw and color only one half of an animal and write its name. Laminate or cover the sheets with clear contact paper and place them in an independent workstation. Invite students to mix-and-match all kinds of creatures.

- Create an "If I Ran the Zoo" bulletin board to display the children's work.

- In science, discuss how the platypus is also unusual because it lays eggs even though it's a mammal.

Animal Mask

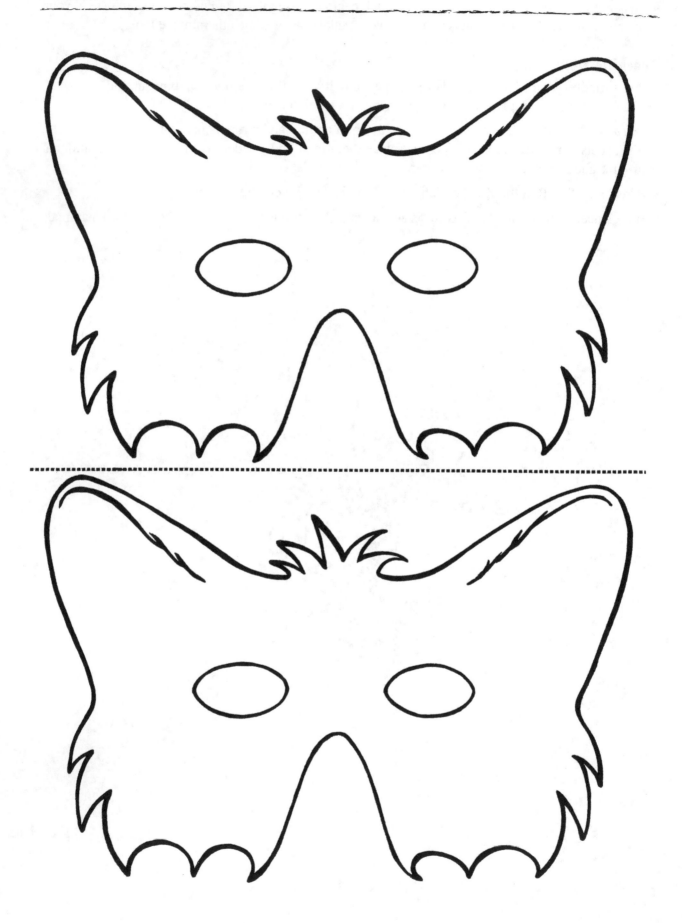

Animals, Animals, Animals
I Want a Pet

Benchmarks/Standards covered:
- Choose a topic for writing.
- Write with a clear purpose and audience in mind.
- Use personal pronouns.
- Write letters or invitations that include relevant information.

Books to explore:

The Best Pet of All by David LaRochelle (Dutton Children's Books, 2004)

The Perfect Pet by Margie Palantini (Katherine Tegen Books, 2003)

Pinky and Rex and the Just-Right Pet by James Howe (Aladdin, 2002)

Arthur's Pet Business by Marc Brown (Little, Brown, 1993)

Bark and Tim: A True Story of Friendship by Audrey Glassman Vernick, Ellen Glassman Gidaro, Tim Brown (Overmountain Press, 2003)

Discussion:

Writing has many purposes. We write to remember things, to share experiences, to learn, and to entertain. Sometimes, we also write to convince someone to think a certain way. This kind of writing is called persuasive writing. Good persuasive writing does at least two things. First, it tells us what we should do or how we should feel. And, secondly, it tells us *why*. For example, a writer might write (Write the following on the board): *I think my parents should buy me a new bike. I think they should do this because I'm too big for my old bike. My knees are all scrunched up when I try to ride and that's not safe.* What are some other good reasons the writer could use to convince his or her parents to buy a new bike? (Add these reasons to the example.) Would "You should buy me a new bike because I *want* one" be a good reason? It might be, but it probably wouldn't convince parents! Good persuasive writing gives the reader logical explanations or reasons that support what the writer wants.

Now it's your turn:

Today, you're going to get the chance to convince your parents that you deserve to get a pet. If you already have a pet, convince your parents to let you have another one or to get a really unusual pet. The first thing you need to do is decide which animal would make the perfect pet. Next, brainstorm all the good reasons you can think of why your parents should let you get one. Get creative! For instance, maybe a grizzly bear would make a good guard. You could ride a horse everywhere and that would save the family gas money. A pig could eat all the family's leftovers, and a tarantula could scare away bad guys.

After you've made your list, pick out your most convincing reasons and write your parents a letter.

Reminders for student writers:

- Remember to start off strong. Let your readers know right away what you want. You could write: Dear Mom and Dad, I want this animal. This animal would make a good pet because ....

- Give at least three good reasons why you deserve this pet or why you think the animal would make a good pet.

- Try to imagine what your parents would say and turn their arguments to your favor. If you think your mom would say, "Dogs shed too much," you might write: Think about how strong your arms will be from vacuuming everyday!

Teaching tips:

- Make a graph about which animals the students already have or would like to have as pets.

- Encourage parents to write their child a letter back.

- Challenge students to pick a common pet, such as a dog or cat, and write a persuasive paragraph about why it's *not* a good choice as a pet.

- Invite an unusual pet and its owner to the classroom for a visit.

Animals, Animals, Animals
Who Am I Talking About?

Benchmarks/Standards covered:
- Use end punctuation correctly, including question marks, exclamation points, and periods.
- Use descriptive words and phrases.
- List questions about essential elements from text (e.g.: why, who, where, what, when, and how) and identify answers.

Books to explore:

ABC Animal Riddles by Susan Joyce (Peel Productions, 1999)
Pig Giggles and Rabbit Rhymes: A Book of Animal Riddles by Mike Downs (Chronicle, 2002)
Who Am I? Wild Animals by Alain Crozen (Chronicle, 2002)
The Little Big Book of Animals by Lena Tabori (Welcome Books, 2002)

Discussion:

One thing writers do is describe characters. They describe what a character looks like and what his or her personality is like. If I asked you to describe what *I* looked like, what would you say? (Let students give numerous responses.) If I asked you to describe my personality, or the way I act and the things I like, what would you say?

Let's play a game. I'm going to describe someone in the room. See if you can guess who I'm talking about. (Describe a child in the room using a variety of physical characteristics and personality traits. If you have time, play a few rounds or allow children to respectfully describe a fellow classmate.)

Now it's your turn:

Animals can make great characters, too. Pick an animal and brainstorm all the things that might describe it. For example, you might write about what color it is or if it has fur or feathers. You could describe the noise it makes or how it moves. After you're done brainstorming, pick your five favorite characteristics and write an animal riddle. On the top of your paper write: The animal I'm thinking of ... (Write this sentence and the following one on the board for students to refer to.) At the bottom of your riddle, write: What animal am I talking about?

Reminders for student writers:

- Think of the unique characteristics of your animal. For example, saying your animal has legs doesn't help us much. But telling us your animal hops on two legs might! Your job isn't to stump your reader; your job is to give your readers good clues.

- You can include clues such as: what your animal eats, where it lives, how it smells, its size, and if its name rhymes with another word.

- Don't forget to write the beginning and ending sentences on the top and bottom of your paper.

Teaching tips:

- Play animal charades.

- On a map, place pins that mark where all the students' animals live. Discuss how animals are native to certain parts of the world.

- Talk about how some animals use camouflage or distinct characteristics (like a horn) to protect themselves.

- Create a bulletin board where an illustration of the animal is posted underneath the riddle so students can "flip and see" if their guesses are correct.

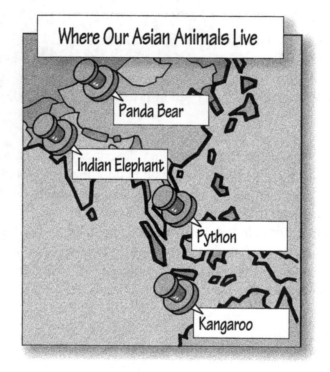

Where Our Asian Animals Live

Panda Bear

Indian Elephant

Python

Kangaroo

Animals, Animals, Animals
Yours Truly

Benchmarks/Standards covered:
- Write a response to literature that demonstrates an understanding of a literary work.
- Dictate or write simple stories.
- Use personal pronouns.

Books to explore:

Dear Mrs. La Rue: Letters from Obedience School by Mark Teague (Scholastic, 2002)

Diary of a Worm by Doreen Cronin (Joanna Cotler, 2003)

Letters from Felix: A Little Rabbit on a World Tour by Annette Langen, Constanza Droop (Parklane Publishing, 2003)

The Jolly Postman by Allan Ahlberg (Little, Brown, 2001)

Discussion:

Have you ever wondered what it's like to be somebody else? Writers get to pretend to be somebody else all the time! Different stories are told from different points of view. A point of view that's used often is first person. If you are telling a story in first person, you, the writer, are speaking directly to the readers. First person is easy to spot. It uses the word "I." *I* did this. *I* said that.

If I wanted to tell the story of Goldilocks in first person, it might sound like this: *One day, I was walking through the words. I came to a door and knocked but no one answered. I walked in and ate up the porridge. Then, I sat in three chairs. (Oops! I broke one!) I was tired, so I tried out a few beds until I found just the right one.*

Now it's your turn:

Instead of writing like Goldilocks or another fairytale character, we're going to be writing as if we're animals at the zoo! First, choose an animal that lives at the zoo. Maybe it's your favorite animal. Maybe it's one you just think would have a good story to tell. Take a few minutes to think about what this animal might say if it could speak in a language we could understand. What would it say about its home? The food? The zookeepers? Zoo visitors? Would it introduce us to its family or tell us about where it used to live? What's the animal's dream or favorite thing to do? What is it afraid of? When you're ready, write a paragraph in first person as that animal. (Younger students may find just a few sentences a big enough challenge.)

Reminders for student writers:

- If you're having trouble writing as an animal, try talking like it for a few minutes. Have a quiet conversation with a classmate; the two of you can practice speaking like your animals.

- Don't forget; first person uses words like "I" and "me" and "my."

- You don't have to tell us only about your life; you can tell us a great story about something that has happened to you at the zoo, too. For example, tell us about the time you almost escaped or a visitor dropped her cotton candy into your cage!

Teaching tips:

- Encourage students to share their work at a zoo party; let them dress up or put on face paint and serve animal crackers.

- Put together a class book called, "At the Zoo: The Inside Story."

- Take a field trip to the zoo or invite a zookeeper to visit.

- Raise money as a class to "adopt" an animal at the zoo.

Animals, Animals, Animals
All About

Benchmarks/Standards covered:
- Recognize the defining characteristics and features of different types of literary forms and genres.
- Use organizational strategies to plan writing.
- Discuss ideas for investigation about a topic or area of personal interest.
- Utilize appropriate searching techniques to gather information from a variety of locations.

Books to explore:

Great Pets! An Extraordinary Guide to More Than 60 Usual and Unusual Family Pets by Sara Bonnett Stein (Storey Books, 2003)

Everything Dog: What Kids Really Want to Know About Dogs by Marty Crisp (Northword Press, 2003)

How Animals Care for Their Babies by Roger B. Hirschland (National Geographic, 1996)

Animals in Winter by Henrietta Bancroft (HarperTrophy, 1997)

Scholastic Encyclopedia of Animals by Laurence Pringle, Norbert Wu (Scholastic, 2001)

Discussion:

Writing that's about things that are made-up is called fiction. Writing that gives readers facts and information, or tells about something that really happened, is called non-fiction. Can anyone give me an example of fiction? (Responses might include picture books, chapter books, a magazine story.) How about non-fiction? (Responses might include: newspaper articles, textbooks, biographies, science books, how-to books.) When you are writing non-fiction, you have a responsibility to tell your readers the truth. This is why research is a big part of writing non-fiction. Research is gathering information and facts. Let's say I want to know all there is to know about taking care of a snake. Where could I find information? (Record answers, which may include: the zoo, library, bookstore, pet store, someone who owns a snake, a herpetologist.)

Now it's your turn:

When an author sits down to write a non-fiction story or article, he or she usually begins with a research plan. Today, we'll be writing our own research plans. (Hand out Research Plan worksheet.) First, you'll need a topic! Chose an animal you know about and would like to know more about. Maybe you'll pick a breed of dog or a cat because you have one at home. Maybe you have a favorite zoo animal you've read or seen a television show about. Next, write all the things you already know about your animal. After you're finished, write down some things you would like to know about your topic. Finally, brainstorm some places where you might go to find the information you need. (Depending on your students' interest or ability, you may have them expand on this lesson by doing the research and writing a report.)

Reminders for student writers:

- Don't worry if you know only a few things about your topic. Researching and finding out more about things is fun!

- Are there other places, other than the ones we listed on the board, where you could go for information? What about a park ranger or a teacher?

Teaching tips:

- Bring in a wide variety of non-fiction books about animals for children to read and explore.

- Discuss how to find/identify a non-fiction book in the library. Go on a non-fiction book scavenger hunt!

- Read one of the "American Girl" books or another historical fiction story. Discuss how this genre combines interesting, true facts about a certain place and time with fictional characters.

- If students do the research and write reports, collect them into a classroom "Animal Encyclopedia." Have them add illustrations.

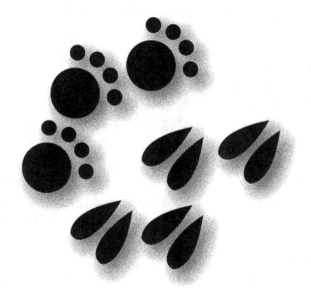

Research Plan

My Topic

Some Facts I Already Know

Three Things I Want to Find Out

Places I Can Look for Information

Workshop Overview:
Time to Celebrate!

Reaching the end of the school year, losing a tooth, going to a birthday party or on a trip—life is filled with all kinds of celebrations, big and small. In "Time to Celebrate," we use these celebrations as a springboard for writing. Students focus on writing complete sentences and using adjectives and nouns. They continue to work on letter writing skills and writing with a purpose and audience in mind. Another skill that is addressed in this workshop is finding the main idea in text. "New Holiday" is a student favorite and gives children a chance to create their own, national holiday. (It also provides you with a great opportunity to discuss other holidays and history.)

Students launch this workshop with a paper clock because it's always time to be creative!

Writing activities	Materials and handouts (one copy for each student)
Class Book	Paper clock A wrapped box with a picture and description of a favorite gift Lucy's Birthday intro transparency Lucy's Birthday worksheet
Tooth Fairy	From the Desk of the Tooth Fairy worksheet Envelopes (optional)
Dear Friend	Writing paper
Postcards	Commercially made blank postcards or tag board cut into homemade postcards
My New Holiday	Press Release worksheet

Time to Celebrate!
Class Book

Benchmarks/Standards covered:
- Use nouns, verbs, and adjectives.
- Write responses to stories by comparing text to other texts or to people or events in their own lives.
- Illustrate writing samples for display and sharing with others.

Books to explore:

Many Luscious Lollipops: A Book About Adjectives by Ruth Heller (Putnam Publishing Group, 1998)

Mama's Perfect Present by Diane Goode (Dutton Children's Books, 1996)

The Thirteen Days of Halloween by Carol Greene (Troll Communications, 2001)

D.W.'s Perfect Present by Marc Brown (Little, Brown, 2004)

Discussion:

(Display your wrapped box.) What do you think is in this box? (Allow children to guess and discuss for a few minutes and then open the box to reveal a picture and description of a favorite gift. Share when and why you received it and who gave it to you.) This is how I would describe this item. (Record a variety of adjectives on the board or overhead.) What do all of these words have in common? They're all adjectives or describing words! Writers use adjectives to give readers details and help paint a vivid picture. What are some things we could describe about an object? (Responses might include: color, size, smell, texture, weight, number.)

Now it's your turn:

Today, you'll have the chance to use some fun adjectives and help make a class book. The book is called "Lucy's Birthday." Let's read the beginning. (Put up Lucy's Birthday intro transparency.) Now, I want you to pretend you are one of Lucy's brothers or sisters. Think about what unique gift you could give her. (Pass out Lucy's Birthday student worksheet.) In the first space, write your name. Next, fill in what you'd give Lucy if you could. Finally, think of at least two adjectives that describe the gift. When you're finished, draw an illustration.

Reminders for student writers:

- Get creative! Try to think of something unusual or makeup a new gift. For example, maybe you could give Lucy a a pink hamster or a machine that will do her homework.

- When you're trying to come up with adjectives, remember what we talked about; adjectives can describe things like an object's color, size, quantity, weight, smell.

- You can write more than two adjectives if you'd like.

- Don't forget to keep your adjectives in mind while you're illustrating the page. In other words, don't make your gift red if you said it was blue!

Teaching tips:

- If possible, make copies of each page and assemble them into a book for each child. This way, children can read along while you read the class book or take a copy home to practice reading.

- Make a list of the students' favorite gifts. Put them into categories and graph their popularity. Extend this activity even further by creating a student "Gift Giving Guide" for parents, other family, and friends.

- Encourage students to write about their own, favorite gift.

Clock

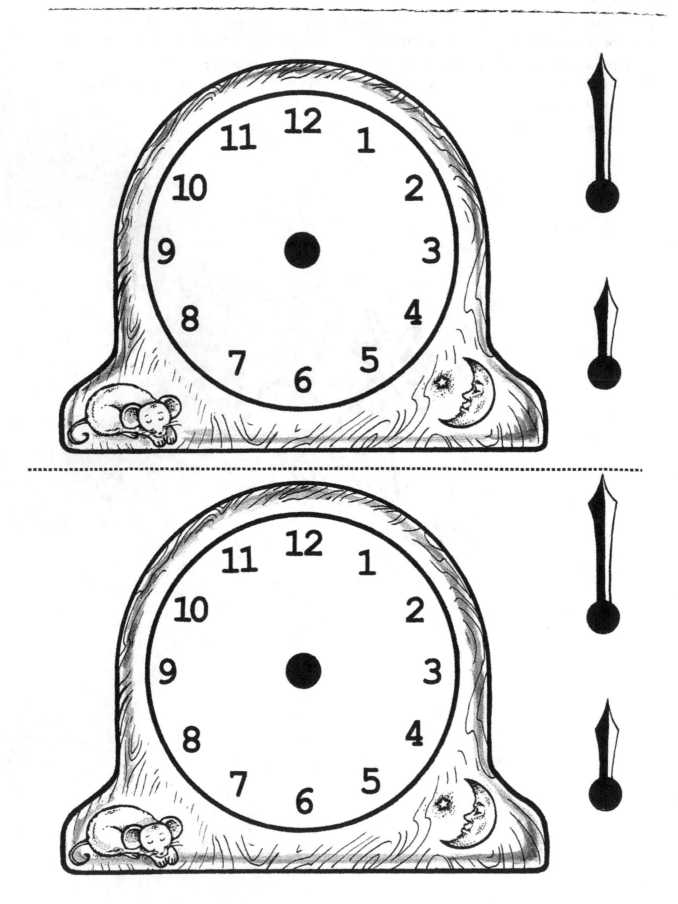

Lucy's Birthday

Do you remember the old lady
who lived in a shoe?
The one with so many children
she didn't know what to do?

Well, this story is about Lucy,
the lady's youngest daughter,
and about the birthday gifts
her brothers and sisters got her.

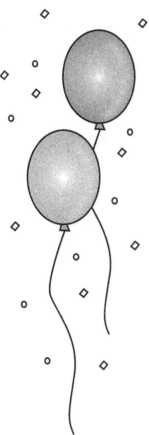

With so many gifts to open,
Lucy had to make a list.
This way she could keep track of
which person gave which gift.

The party was a huge hit;
the guests did nothing but rave.
And with the list Lucy could thank everyone
for the cool stuff they gave …

Lucy's Birthday

_____ gave Lucy a

_____ .

It was _____ .

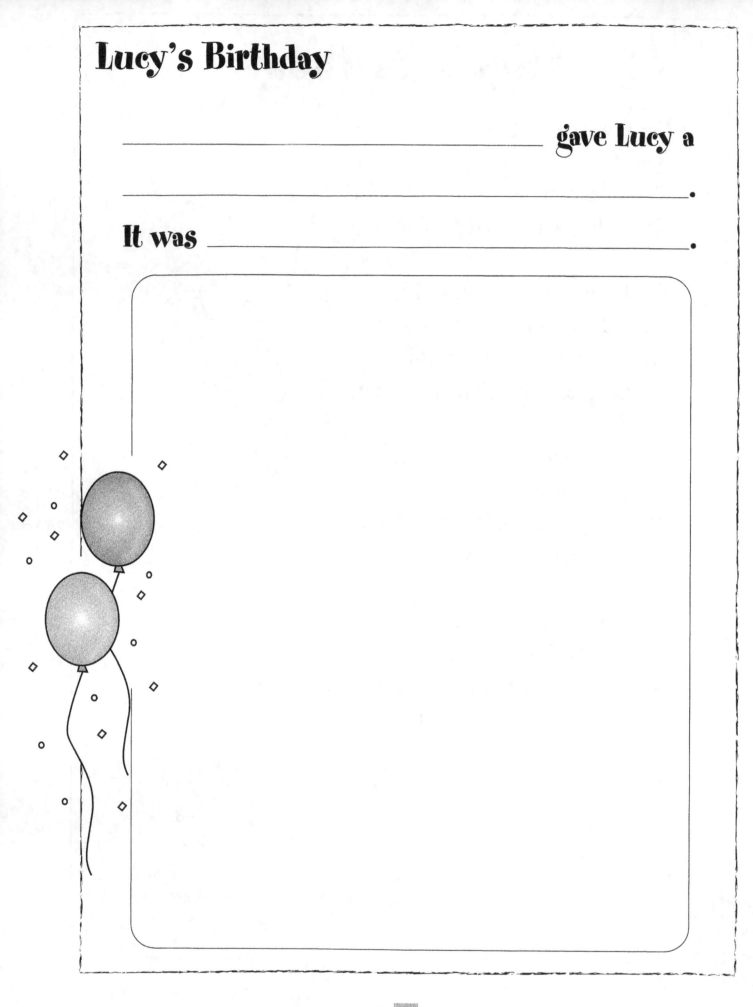

Time to Celebrate
Tooth Fairy

Benchmarks/Standards covered:
- Write letters or invitations that include relevant information and follow letter-writing format.
- Generate ideas for writing through discussion with others.

Books to explore:

How Many Teeth by Paul Showers (HarperTrophy, 1991)
Nice Try, Tooth Fairy by Mary W. Olson (Aladdin, 2003)
What Do the Fairies Do with All Those Teeth? by Michael Luppens (Firefly Books, 1996)
Dear Tooth Fairy by Alan Durnat (Candlewick Press, 2004)
Junie B. Jones: First Grader, Toothless Wonder by Barbara Park (Random House, 2003)

Discussion:

Who has heard of the Tooth Fairy? (Depending on your students and their sensitivity to the subject, you may want to ask the children how many of them have already lost baby teeth.) Have you ever stopped to wonder what she does with all the teeth she collects? Let's brainstorm some possibilities. (Record several ideas on the board for later use.) A good way to find out something you want to know from someone is to ask! And one fun way to ask someone something is to write him or her a letter.

Let's write a letter to the Tooth Fairy and ask her what she does with all the teeth. Our letter will have five important parts: the date, a greeting, the body, a closing, and a signature. (Write the letter on the overhead or board as you discuss each part.) First, we have to write the date so the Tooth Fairy knows when we are writing her. Next, we have to have a greeting. What should our greeting be? (Responses might include: Dear, Hello, Hi, To, Greetings.) And now, we get to the body. The body of the letter tells or asks the reader something. What do we want to tell the Tooth Fairy? What do we want to ask her? Next, we close the letter. A closing can be many things: Sincerely, Thank you, Yours truly, Best regards. Which one should we use? (If you'd like, encourage students to think of other possible closings.) And finally, we need to sign the letter. When you sign your name, it is called your signature. Great job! Let's read our letter together.

Now it's your turn:

Pretend you are the Tooth Fairy and have just received the class letter in your mail. Your assistant is on vacation, so now it's your job to write back! (Hand out From the Desk of the Tooth Fairy worksheet.) Tell us what you do with all the teeth you collect. Be sure to write the letter using the five parts of a letter we talked about: date, greeting, body, closing, signature. (If you haven't done so already, write the five parts on the board for reference.)

Reminders for student writers:

- If you want, give us more information like: what you look like, how you got the job, where you live. Do you have any nicknames or pets or a family?

- Check the board for the five parts of a letter. When you're finished with your letter, make sure it has all four parts.

- Have fun with the signature! Use fancy letters or a special color or marker if you'd like.

Teaching tips:

- Provide envelopes and let students decorate them as part of their From the Desk of The Tooth Fairy stationery.

- Graph how many teeth the students have lost.

- Read *Throw Your Tooth on the Roof: Tooth Traditions from Around the World* by Selby Beeler (Houghton Mifflin, 2001) and explore various world traditions.

- Invite a dentist to visit the classroom.

- Have children sew small "tooth" pillows to hold lost teeth.

From the desk of
the Tooth Fairy

Time to Celebrate
Dear Friend

Benchmarks/Standards covered:
- Write letters or invitations that include relevant information and follow letter format.
- Generate ideas for writing through discussion with others.
- Compare what is heard with prior knowledge and experience.

Books to explore:

The Jolly Postman by Allan Ahlberg (Little, Brown, 2001)

Dear Peter Rabbit and Yours Truly, Goldilocks by Alma Flor Ada (Aladdin, 1997 & 2001)

Dear Annie by Judith Casely (HarperTrophy, 1994)

Dear Mr. Blueberry by Simon James (Aladdin, 1996)

The Post Office Book: Mail and How It Moves by Gail Gibbons (HarperTrophy, 1986)

Discussion:

Do you remember when you started school this year? How did you feel? Were you nervous or excited, or a little of both? What kind of questions did you have? What were you most worried about? (Spend some time letting children share their "beginning of the school year" stories. Record a variety of their responses on the board.) Now that you're expert first graders (or appropriate grade), what advice would you give to someone who is just coming into this grade? What would you tell them about the classroom rules or about me as their teacher? What activity has been your favorite? Which subject is the most challenging or the most fun? (Record students' responses to these questions as well.)

Now it's your turn:

Yay! It's the end of the school year—at least in our imaginations! Because you're now the expert, I would like you to write a letter of advice to a child who is coming into this classroom. Take a look at what we've recorded on the board or feel free to brainstorm more advice. Really think about what might be most important to know about being a first grader. Are there any "inside tips" you could share? After you decide on a few pieces of advice or tips, begin your letter. Remember to include the five parts of a letter: date, greeting, body, closing, and your signature. (You may want to write these five parts on the board again for reference.)

Reminders for student writers:

- Since I don't know the names of the children who will be in my class next year, please begin the letter with Dear Friend.

- Remember, your job is to help an incoming student feel *good* about being in first grade. Don't go overboard about how challenging a certain subject or unit is; make sure you spend time sharing some positive things too!

- Think about the kinds of things you would liked to have known at the beginning of the year.

Teaching tips:

- Compile all the letters of advice into a book and put copies on the desks at the beginning of the new school year.

- Expand on the activity by asking students to write letters of advice about other things they might know about like: becoming a big brother or sister, riding a bike, losing a tooth, being a good friend, being a new student.

- Have students write letters of advice (or write a class letter) to a fictional character who has a problem. For example, what would students tell Alexander in Judith Viorst's *Alexander and the Terrible, Horrible, No Good, Very Bad Day* (Aladdin, 1976)?

Time to Celebrate!
Postcards

Benchmarks/Standards covered:
- Tell the main idea of a selection that has been read aloud.
- Develop a main idea for writing.
- Write letters or invitations that include relevant information and follow letter format.

Books to explore:

Postcards from Pluto: A Tour of the Solar System by Loreen Leedy (Holiday House, 1996)
Postcards from Brazil by Zoe Dawson (Steck-Vaughn, 1995)
Stringbean's Trip to the Shining Sea by Vera B. and Jennifer Williams (Greenwillow, 1988)

Discussion:

We've been having fun writing letters lately. Letters are a great way to share information, but what if you don't have time to write a long letter? What can you do, for example, if you don't have a phone or computer to write an e-mail but you still want to tell somebody something? One thing you might try is to write a postcard. Who knows what a postcard is? Has anyone ever received one? (Hold up a postcard, either one you've received or a blank one.) As you can see, there's not much space to write on a postcard! This is why, when you're writing a postcard, you have to keep things short and get to the main idea. The main idea of any piece of writing is the one thing you want your readers to know or take away. This doesn't mean you can't give a few details, but you won't be able to tell a long, descriptive story. Here's an example. (Read or write the following on the board:

> July 4th,
>
> Dear Mom and Dad,
>
> I'm having a great time at Cedar Point. It's THE place for roller coaster lovers! Everywhere you look, there is a new ride. In fact, there are so many roller coasters that I bet it will take two days to go on them all.
>
> I hope you are well. See you soon.
>
> Your son,
> Matthew

What is the author's main point? (That Cedar Point has lots of roller coasters.)

Now it's your turn:

I want you to imagine you've just won a trip to someplace you've always wanted to go (or return to). Write a postcard to someone back home, telling him or her about a highlight of your trip. Let's brainstorm some places we'd like to visit and what we might see there. (As a class, make a list of destinations and their attractions that kids would like to see or places they've been.) Figure out what your main idea will be and include this one thing you want to make sure your readers know. Next, write your postcard. (Hand out blank postcards.) When you're finished, turn the postcard over and draw a picture of your trip or yourself enjoying an attraction.

Reminders for student writers:

- Even though it is shorter than a regular letter, your postcard needs a date, greeting, body, closing, and signature.

- Read your postcard to a neighbor. See if he or she can figure out your main idea.

Teaching tips:

- Incorporate state history by having students create postcards that highlight their state or a state attraction.

- Keep a collection of postcards from places where children have gone during vacation breaks. Ask parents and other family members who will be traveling to send a postcard to the class.

- Discuss other forms or older forms of communication such as cave drawings, smoke signals, drums, Morse Code, sign language, etc.

Time to Celebrate!
My New Holiday

Benchmarks/Standards covered:

- List questions about essential elements (e.g.: why, who, where, what, when, and how) from text and identify answers.
- Determine purpose and audience for writing.
- Follow multi-step oral directions.

Books to explore:

Kids Around the World Celebrate: The Best Feasts and Festivals From Many Lands by Lynda Jones (Wiley, 1999)

Lights of Winter: Winter Celebrations Around the World by Heather Conrad (Lightport Books, 2001)

Do You Know What Day Tomorrow Is? A Teacher's Almanac by Lee Bennett Hopkins (Citation Press, 1975)

Discussion:

Holidays are special days. Who can give me an example of a holiday? Why do you think we have holidays? (Responses might include: for fun, to remember a special date or person.) What are some ways people celebrate holidays? (Record answers, which might include: taking the day off, fireworks, eating cakes or other special foods, playing music, dancing, throwing parades, giving gifts.) People who thought a special day was needed to celebrate or remember something or someone started many of our holidays. Often, the very first step was telling people about their idea.

Now it's your turn:

What new holiday would you create if you could? Today, you're going to have the chance to do just that. Invent a new, national holiday for people to celebrate. Maybe you think there should be a Wear Mismatched Socks Day or Eat With Your Fingers Day. Perhaps, you think everyone should have a day off to do nothing but read. (If you have kindergartners or first graders, you might want to spend some time brainstorming as a class and recording their ideas on the board.) Once you've decided on a new holiday and how it should be celebrated, it'll be your job to tell other people about it. One way people tell other people news is through a press release. A press release is a short paragraph or two that you send to a newspaper about a news item. Businesses and people send press releases when they have news to share. They tell the "what, who, when, why, and how" of a story. (Hand out Press Release worksheets.)

Reminders for student writers:

- In the "what" line, write the name of your holiday.

- In the "who" line, write who should be celebrating the holiday. Everyone? Just kids? Americans? Everyone in the world?

- In the "when" line, write the day or date of your holiday.

- In the "where" line, tell us if there's any special place people should go to celebrate. For example, is the celebration at a park, downtown, or at your house?

- In the "why" line, tell us why you think your holiday is important. You can also tell us how you came up with the idea.

- In the "how" line, tell readers how the holiday is to be celebrated.

Teaching tips:

- Encourage older students to write a newspaper story about the new holiday.

- Pick a few of the do-able ones (or have a random drawing) and celebrate a few of the student-created holidays! As a class, write a press release to send to the other classrooms in your school about the event.

Press Release

★★ For Immediate Release ★★

What (My new holiday): _____

_____

Who: _____

_____

When: _____

_____

Where: _____

_____

Why: _____

_____

How: _____

_____

Workshop Overview: Let's Play

Play is children's work. Play is also a great way to motivate young writers! This workshop, like the others in this book, is about having fun with words. The workshop starts off with a simple activity where children use visual aids (sports pictures) to write a caption. Writing captions is a great way to practice proper subject-verb sentence structure as well as finding a main idea. Students get the chance to use various resources to enhance vocabulary and to illustrate their writing, too.

To promote the feeling of "we're in this together," I like to give students a team shirt to decorate. A nice extension to this is to, as a class, come up with a team name. For example, the Wild Writers or Pen Pals.

Writing activities	Materials and handouts (one copy for each student)
Sport Caption	Team "shirt" Variety of sport pictures cut from magazines and newspapers
Toy Ad	Thesaurus for each student (optional) Toy Ad worksheet
Roller Coaster Poem	Large drawing paper
My Marvelous Machine	My Marvelous Machine worksheet
Rulebook	Writing paper

Let's Play
Sport Caption

Benchmarks/Standards covered:
- Use visual aids as sources to gain additional information.
- Use nouns, verbs, and adjectives.
- Use conventions of punctuation and capitalization in written work.

Books to explore:

To Root to Toot to Parachute: What Is a Verb? By Brian P. Cleary (Carolrhoda, 2001)
Add It Dip It Fix It: A Book of Verbs by R.M. Schneider (Houghton Mifflin, 1995)
Shake, Rattle and Roll: An Action-Packed Verb Book by Keith R. Potter with Ken Fulk (Chronicle Books, 1999)

Discussion:

(To begin the lesson, hold up a sports picture that includes lots of action. Close your eyes or hold the picture so you cannot see it.) Good writers can paint pictures in the minds of their readers. I know you all are good writers, so what would you tell me if I asked you to describe what's happening in this picture? (Record the students' answers on the board or overhead.) Hmm. Take a look at your answers. Do you see what I see? Your descriptions use verbs. Verbs are words that show action. (Underline the verbs.) Can anyone think of some more verbs? What kind of actions might you see in sports? (As a class, make a list of sports-related verbs. For example: throw, run, jump, skate, flip, kick.) Writers describe photographers' photos all the time. Those brief descriptions below a picture are called captions.

Now it's your turn:

Everyone is going to write a caption today. In a moment, I will be passing out a picture.* When you get yours, take a few minutes to study it. Pretend you have to describe what's happening in the picture to someone else in only one sentence. What is the action? What are the people *doing*? If you have trouble, check back with the list of verbs we brainstormed as a class. When you're ready, glue your photo on a piece of paper and write your description, or caption, below. Share it with a neighbor; can they pick out your verb?

Reminders for student writers:

- Don't forget to start your sentence with a capital letter and end it with a period.
- Try to use exciting verbs. Is the person in your photo leaping or speeding or pounding the ball?
- Is there more than one thing happening at the same time? Go ahead and use more than one verb.

Teaching tips:

- *If you have the resources, allow students to find and cut out their own sports picture or photo from old magazines or newspapers.

- A variation: bring in sports photos and have students imagine what the people in the photo are thinking or saying. Have them create thought bubbles using sticky-notes and put them on the photographs.

- Load the class library with many sports-related books or biographies of athletes.

- Encourage children to read the captions in newspapers and magazines and bring in examples to share.

- Have fun trying out exciting verbs in the classroom. For example, instead of walking to their seats, tell them to tip-toe or slink.

Team Shirt

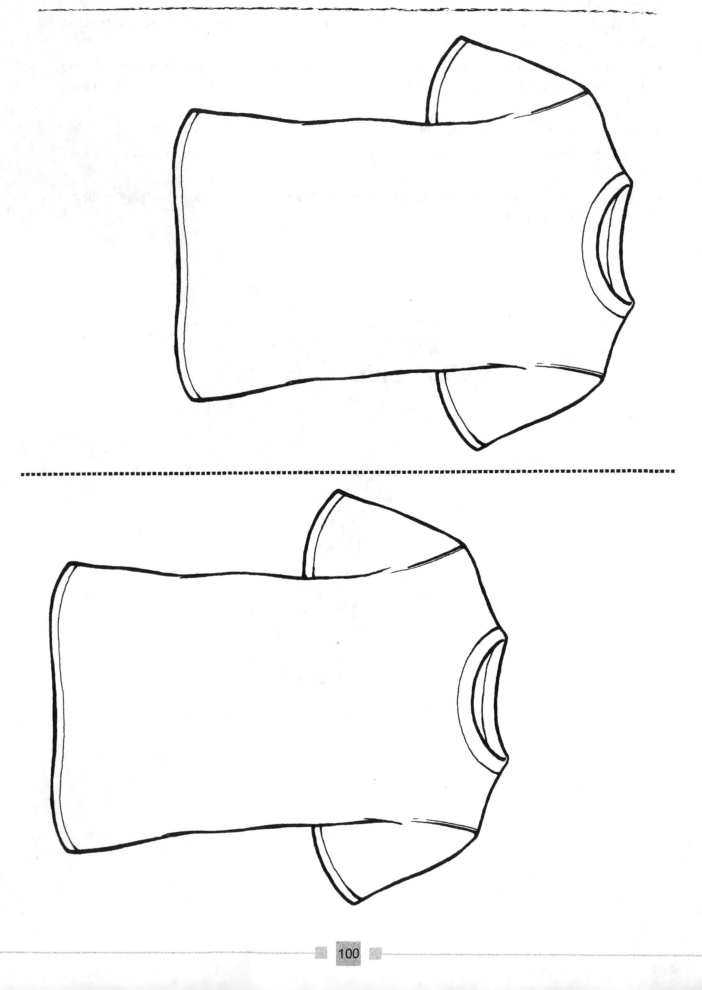

Let's Play
Toy Ad

Benchmarks/Standards covered:
- Explain how an author's word choice and use of methods affect the reader.
- Compose writings that convey a clear message and include well-chosen details.
- Determine purpose and audience for writing.
- Use a variety of resources to enhance vocabulary.

Books to explore:

Hairy, Scary, Ordinary: What is an Adjective? by Brian P. Cleary (Carolrhoda Books, 2000)
Scholastic's Children's Thesaurus (Scholastic, 1998)
Tub Toys by Terry Miller Shannon and Timothy Warner (Tricycle Press, 2002)

Discussion:

I want you to think about your favorite toy. Think about when you got it. Who gave it to you? Was it a gift? Or did you buy it with your own money? Chances are good that it was something you asked for. How do we usually know about new toys? (Responses might include: we see someone else with one, we see it in the store, we see a commercial or see an advertisement.) Many things are sold through ads. Advertisements can be commercials on television or pictures in magazines or newspapers. (If you have time, ask students to share their favorite ad.) An ad's job is to sell something. How? Usually by doing three things: showing the thing they want to sell, telling people about the product, and telling people how their lives would be better if they had it. Ads often use lively language. If an ad said, "This toy car is fun," you might buy it. But if the ad said, "This toy car is a blast!" you would probably be more interested, right? One way to find interesting words is to look in a special book called a thesaurus. If you look up a word in a thesaurus, it will tell you some other words that mean pretty much the same thing you might use instead. For example, let's look up the word big. Instead of big, you might use: giant, large, huge, grand, great, vast.

Now it's your turn:

Today we're going to write an advertisement for our favorite toys. (Hand out Toy Ad worksheets.) Remember, ads have a job to do. On your worksheet, there are places for you to 1) show the toy 2) tell readers about the toy, and 3) tell readers why they should buy the toy. Also, remember what we talked about. Lively words are more likely to get a reader's attention. Try to use exciting adjectives. Think about words that would get *you* to consider buying a toy.

Reminders for student writers:

- If you get stuck or want to find a more exciting word, try a thesaurus.

- Ads usually use lively *colors,* too. Use your markers or crayons to liven up your artwork.

- You need to think of at least five adjectives to describe your toy. You may use more if you'd like.

- Have fun and get creative with the reasons why someone should have a toy like yours. Will it make them laugh so hard they get the hiccups? Will the toy make family and friends actually turn green with envy?

Teaching tips:

- Encourage students to read their ads out loud, with energy and expression. Ask them to consider why using a "lively voice" might help sell a product, too.

- Discuss what it means to be a consumer and how to be a wiser one. Have kids keep a commercial diary for 30 minutes one night. Ask them to name the product that's being sold and if the advertisement worked. ("Yes, it made me want to buy it. No, it didn't make me want to buy it.")

- Have a "Bring Your Favorite Toy to School" Day.

Let's Play
Roller Coaster Poem

Benchmarks/Standards covered:
- Use descriptive words and phrases.
- Dictate or write informal writings for various purposes.
- Deliver brief informal descriptive presentations recalling an event or personal experience that convey relevant information and descriptive details.
- Use a variety of resources to enhance vocabulary.

Books to explore:
Roller Coaster by Marla Frazee (Harcourt Children's Book, 2003)
Harriet and the Roller Coaster by Nancy Carlson (Carolrhoda Books, 2003)
The Way I Feel by Janan Cain (Parenting Press, 2000)
Today I Feel Silly and Other Moods that Make My Day by Jamie Lee Curtis (Joanna Cotler, 1998)

Discussion:
(Before beginning the lesson, draw several circle faces with various expressions on the board. For example, happy, bored, angry, scared, sleepy.) Pictures can give us a lot of information. What feelings are these faces showing? What are some other feelings not shown on these faces? (Record students' answers for later use.) Good writers know that it's important to tell how a character is feeling. Readers can relate to a character who feels the same kinds of things they do. Sometimes writers show feelings by describing what a character is doing. For example, if we read, "The boy screamed and covered his face with his hands," we'd probably think the boy was scared. If we read, "The girl smiled and jumped up and down," we'd probably think she was happy.

Here's a funny thing about feelings; sometimes you feel all kinds of feelings all at once! Has that ever happened to anyone? One thing that causes people to feel all kinds of feelings at once, or causes different people to feel different things, is a roller coaster ride. Who's ever been on a roller coaster? (Allow students to share for a few minutes.)

Now it's your turn:
We're going to practice writing about feelings today by creating a roller coaster poem. The first things we need, of course, are roller coasters! When I give you a piece of paper, I want you to draw a roller coaster. (Hand out drawing paper.) Now, don't get too carried away with your drops, loops, twists, and turns! After you have a roller coaster, pretend you are going for a ride. Above each part of the coaster, show your reader how you are feeling by either writing the name of the feeling or describing what is happening. For instance, at the beginning of your roller coaster maybe you could write, "My heart is pounding." Or maybe you could just write "Nervous." At the top of a hill, you could write "Scared" or "I'm screaming." (Draw your own roller coaster on the board or overhead and demonstrate. Write your words "along the tracks.")

Reminders for student writers:

- *Show* feelings during at least one part of your roller coaster ride. (Younger students probably have an easier time just naming a feeling. Challenge older students to write physical descriptions at more sections of their roller coaster ride.)

- If you need an idea for a feeling, look back at the list we made together on the board.

- Don't forget to write about how you feel when the ride comes to an end.

Teaching tips:

- Create a "Rollicking Roller Coaster Romp" bulletin board and write, as a class, about the various feelings the class might experience on a ride. You could also write a class story about a day at an amusement park.

- Play Guess the Feeling Charades.

- Ask the students, "How do you feel when your turn on a ride is over? Glad or Sad?" Graph the results.

- Roller coasters are a great introduction to gravity and G-force. Explore these concepts during science.

Let's Play
My Marvelous Machine

Benchmarks/Standards covered:
- Compare what is heard to prior knowledge or experience.
- Write labels for objects.
- Illustrate writing samples for display and for sharing with others.

Books to explore:

Marvelous Mud Washing Machine by Patty Wolcott (HarperCollins, 1974)
Mr. Murphy's Marvelous Invention by Eileen Christelow (Houghton Mifflin, 1983)
The Marvelous Toy by Tom Paxton (HarperCollins, 1996)

Discussion:

Who likes to do chores? Me neither! Sometimes, when people have a chore to do, they come up with an invention to do the work. For instance, Eli Whitney wanted to help cotton farmers. Pulling cotton balls and the tiny seeds apart from each other was hard, boring work so, in 1793, Whitney invented the cotton gin to do the job. Who can think of some other useful inventions we use everyday? (Responses might include: washing machine, automobile, telephone, microwave.) Why do you think people invented these machines? (Responses might include: to make life easier, safer.)

Now it's your turn:

What jobs or chores do you have? (Write some of the responses on the board.) Today, we're going to invent a marvelous machine to do a job we don't like or need help doing. (Hand out My Marvelous Machine worksheet.) First, make a sketch of your marvelous machine and give it a name. Next, tell us about what the machine does and how it works. Let's say, you want to invent a Room Cleaning Machine. Do you have to turn it on with a switch or crank it up? Does it make any weird noise while it's working? Does it have any special features? For example, does it also "beep" when it's done cleaning or take out the trash for you?

Reminders for student writers:

- If you can't think of a chore, check the list on the board.
- Eli Whitney wanted to help farmers. If you can't think of a job *you'd* like help with, think of a marvelous machine *others* could use.
- We've been practicing labels and captions in Writing Club; don't forget to label the parts of your marvelous machine.
- Be sure to tell us *why* you invented the machine. Was the job boring, hard, dangerous, time consuming?
- Include what you will do with all the extra time you'll have.

Teaching tips:

- Read more about Eli Whitney, the cotton gin, or other important inventions and their inventors.

- Ask the students to vote for the modern day invention they use or like the most. Graph the results. Continue to expand on this by asking them to give up a modern day invention/convenience for one day and write about the experience.

- Play the song "The Marvelous Toy" by Tom Paxton. Have students use their imaginations to draw the toy.

My Marvelous Machine

My name of my marvelous machine is:_____.

I invented it because_____

_____.

You turn it on by_____.

Some of my marvelous machine's special features are:_____

_____.

Now that I have extra time, I'm going to_____

_____.

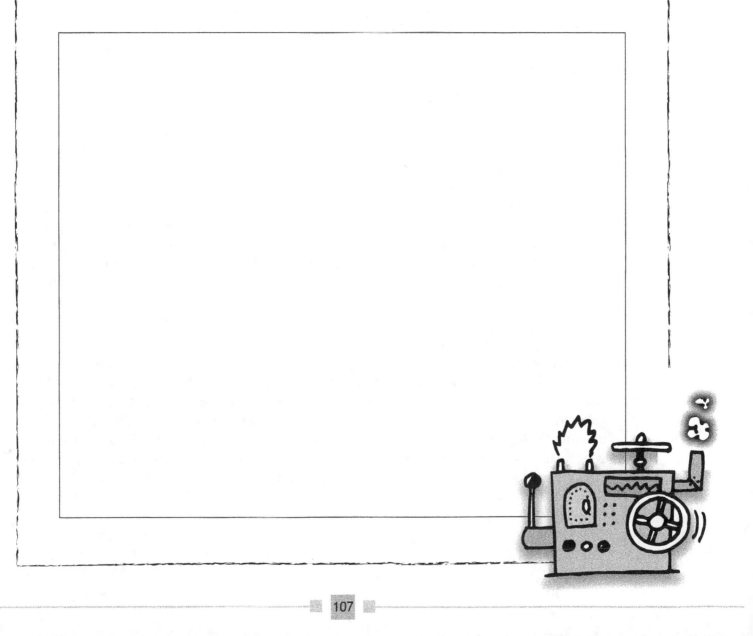

Let's Play
Rulebook

Benchmarks/Standards covered:
- Choose a topic for writing.
- Construct complete sentences with subjects and verbs.
- Apply tools to judge the quality of writing.
- Reread own writing.

Books to explore:

The Illustrated Rules of Football by R.L. Patey (Ideals Children's Books, 2001)
Hopscotch, Hangman, Hot Potato and Ha Ha Ha: A Rulebook of Children's Games by Jack Macguire (Fireside, 1990)
It's a Rule by Jeri S. Cipriano (Yellow Umbrella Books, 2003)
Let the Games Begin by Maya Ajmeru and Michael J. Regan (Charlesbridge Publishing, 2000)

Discussion:

Good writers always ask, "What would happen if?" For a few minutes, I want you to think about what would happen if there were no rules in our classroom. That might sound like a fun idea, but what do you suppose it would be like if everyone just did anything they wanted? (Allow the children to discuss this for a few minutes.) So why are rules important? (Help students see that rules help keep everyone safe.) One way we can make sure everyone knows the rules is to write them down. (Point out any posted classroom rules.) Since we've been talking about games and sports during this Writing Club workshop, let's pretend we've been asked to write the rules for kickball. (Write "kickball" on the board as well as the rest of the information. Write the rules in complete sentences.) First, let's write what the object, or goal, of the game is. (The object of kickball is to score more points than the other team.) Next, let's write the rules. (Responses might include: If you get three strikes, you're out. You can't throw the ball at someone's head. If another player catches a kicked ball, you're out.)

Now it's your turn:

Now, I'd like for you to pick a game or sport you like to play and know about. It will be your job to write about the object of the game and a few of its rules. Follow the format we used as a class. First, write the name of your game down. Second, write the object or the goal of the game. And third, write a few of the rules. You need to think of at least three. (You might want to write: Name, Object, and Rules on the board for the students to refer to.) Make sure all of your sentences are complete sentences. In other words, they have a subject and a verb. A good writer always goes back and makes sure he has met his writing goal, so when you're done, go through the checklist on the board.

Reminders for student writers:

- When you're finished, go back and read through your work. You want to make sure your rules are clear, so look at the checklist I've written on the board. Ask yourself, "Did I ..."

- Write the name of my game or sport?

- Write the object of the game in a complete sentence?

- Write at least three rules in complete sentence form?

- Have all my sentences begin with a capital letter and end with a period?

Teaching tips:

- Put the students' work together and create a class "Recess Rulebook."

- Go outside and play a game where one of the rules is changed. For example, play kickball and have the kids run the bases in reverse order. Play baseball and give players five chances to hit the ball instead of three.

- Explore games from other parts of the world. Here is a good site that gives examples of games played around the world. <http://www.topics-mag.com/edition11/games-section.htm>

Workshop Overview:
Spy Time

Who doesn't love a good mystery or search for treasure? In this workshop, the Benchmarks/Standards covered include going on a scavenger hunt to find fun words to add to their writing, and finding rhyming words to use in a classroom game called I Spy A Rhyme Time. They will also be writing questions and using deductive reasoning to solve riddles. Other activities include re-telling stories and putting them in sequence, which is an important step in making an outline. The workshop finishes up with a classroom favorite, writing Round-Robin stories!

To get kids in the spirit of looking at words and writing in a different way, I like to give each of them a magnifying glass made of tag board at the beginning of each Writing Club.

Writing activities	Materials and handouts (one copy for each student)
Word Hunt	Tag Board Magnifying Glasses Clipboards (optional)
Mixed Up Fairy Tales	Goldilocks and Three Bears transparency Fairy Tale Puzzle worksheet
I Spy a Rhyme Time	Rhyming dictionaries (optional)
What Is It?	Small gift bags or envelopes
Round-Robin Stories	Writing paper

Spy Time
Word Hunt

Benchmarks/Standards covered:
- Print legibly using appropriate spacing.
- Create phonetically-spelled written work that can usually be read by the writer and others.
- Use various resources to enhance vocabulary.
- Understand the role of an author.

Books to explore:

Junie B. Jones and Some Sneeky Peeky Spying by Barbara Park (Random House for Young Readers, 1994)

Pooh's Scavenger Hunt by Isabel Gaines (Random House/Disney, 1998)

I Spy Treasure Hunt: A Book of Picture Riddles by Jean Marzollo and Walter Wick (Scholastic, 1999)

Harriet the Spy by Lousie Fitzhugh (Yearling, reprint 2001)

Discussion:

Good writers know using a variety of words can make their work interesting. This is why some writers collect words, keeping fun, useful, or unusual words in a special notebook to use later in their writing. How do writers find new words to add to their collection? Usually they just have their eyes and ears open as they go through their day. For example, they might read a neat word in a book or the newspaper or overhear someone talking at the store.

Today, we'll be using our eyes and ears and our other senses to collect words in a special way. How many of you have ever been on a scavenger hunt? Well, we're going on a special kind of quest—a word hunt.

Now it's your turn:

In a few moments, I will ask you to find a spot and start collecting. First, sit down and look around. Write down what you see. Don't write sentences; make a list. Maybe you'll collect an object or a color. Next, use your nose to collect words that have to do with what you smell. Use your hands to collect words for what you feel. Finally, close your eyes and sit quietly. Listen for any sounds and then write down what you hear. (If possible, provide students with a special notebook or let them make their own and decorate the cover. When ready, dismiss students from their seats.)

Reminders for student writers:

- Try to collect words you think no one else will have on their list.

- Don't worry about whether or not your words are good; just write down your ideas.

- When you're finished, organize your words by putting them into categories. Some categories might be: things I heard, things I saw. Come up with your own system.

Teaching tips:

- If possible, give students plenty of time to sit quietly in a space, alone. Consider going outside for your word hunt. Going outside is a great way to collect nature words to use in a haiku.

- Create a bulletin board of "Fun and Unusual Words" that students can refer to while writing. Encourage students to keep adding to it.

Magnifying Glasses

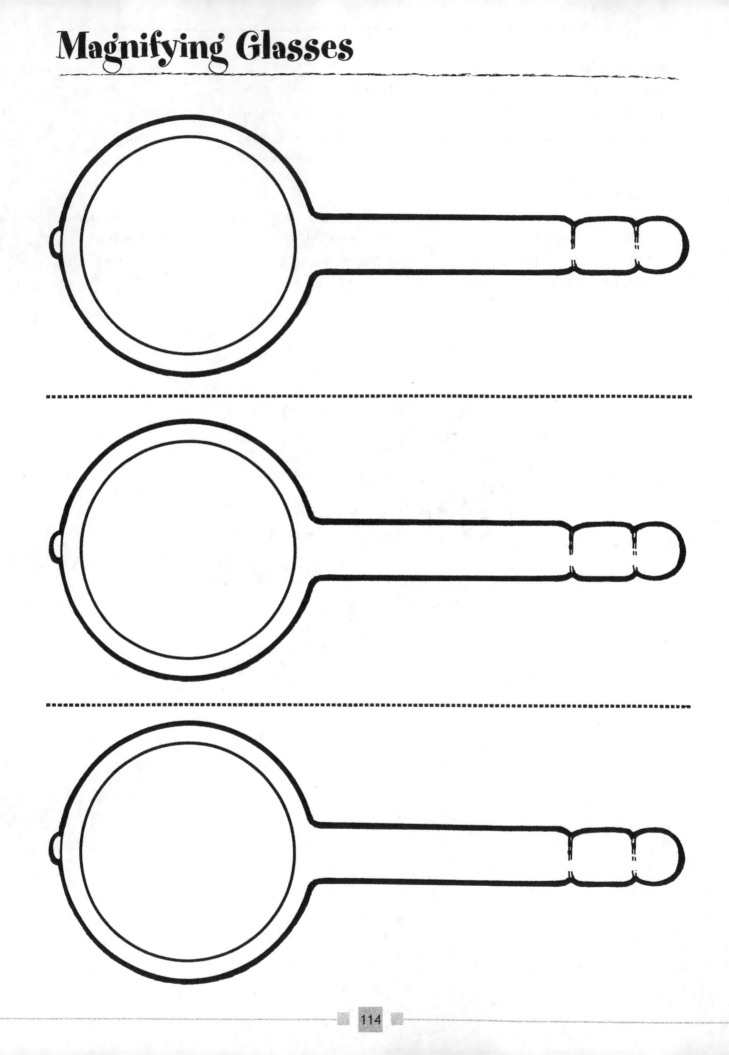

Spy Time
Mixed Up Fairy Tales

Benchmarks/Standards covered:
- Recall information from a story by sequencing pictures and events.
- Distinguish between stories, poems, plays, fairy tales, and fables.
- Apply tools to judge the quality of writing.

Books to explore:

Classic Fairy Tales by Scott Gustafson (The Greenwich Workshop Press, 2003)

The Random House Book of Fairy Tales by Amy Ehrlich (Random House Books for Young Readers, 2000)

Aesop's Fables by Aesop, retold by Jerry Pinkney (SeeStar Books, 2000)

The Golden Book of Fairy Tales by Marie Ponsot (Golden Books, 1999)

Discussion:

(Open lesson by reading a favorite fairy tale. A "fractured fairy tale," one where there is a funny or modern twist, would also work well.) Who can re-tell the story we just read? What happened at the beginning of the story? In the middle? At the end? Being able to remember and retell a story in the right order are important skills to have if you are a storyteller! Do you know why this is? Let's try an experiment. (Put up Goldilocks and the Three Bears transparency.) At the bottom of the page is the story of Goldilocks and Three Bears. It's all mixed up, though. (Read story in mixed up order.) Let's see if we can unscramble the story and put the pieces together in the right order. (Work as a class to put story sections into right order and write inside puzzle pieces.) What have we learned about telling a story in the right order? (Stories don't make sense if told out of order.)

Now it's your turn:

Today, you're going to have the chance to have a little mixed up fairly tale fun. (Pass out Fairy Tale Puzzle worksheet.) First, choose a fairy tale you're familiar with. On a piece of sloppy copy paper, write five things that happen in the story. Be sure to include the story's beginning and its ending. You'll also need to write three things that happen during the middle of the story. Once you've decided which scenes, or parts, to include, write them in the puzzle pieces on your worksheet. Put one sentence in each puzzle piece. Next, cut the puzzle pieces out and trade your puzzle with a neighbor's puzzle. See if you can put each other's mixed up fairy tale in order.

Reminders for student writers:

- Put your name or initials on the back of each puzzle piece before trading them. This way, we can find out where lost pieces belong.
- Be sure to fill in each puzzle piece; don't leave any blank.

- After you've put together your neighbor's puzzle, read it quietly and ask yourself, "Does this make sense?"

Teaching tips:

- If possible, provide students with small, plastic baggies to store puzzle pieces.

- Collect all the puzzles and put them in a special reading/writing center for children to visit.

- Share a fractured fairy tale; encourage children to write their own by changing a detail or event on one of their puzzle pieces.

- If you have any old books that are falling apart, don't toss them. Find a new use for them! Carefully remove pages and cover or cut off the page numbers. Mix them up and let students put them back in the right order.

Goldilocks Transparency

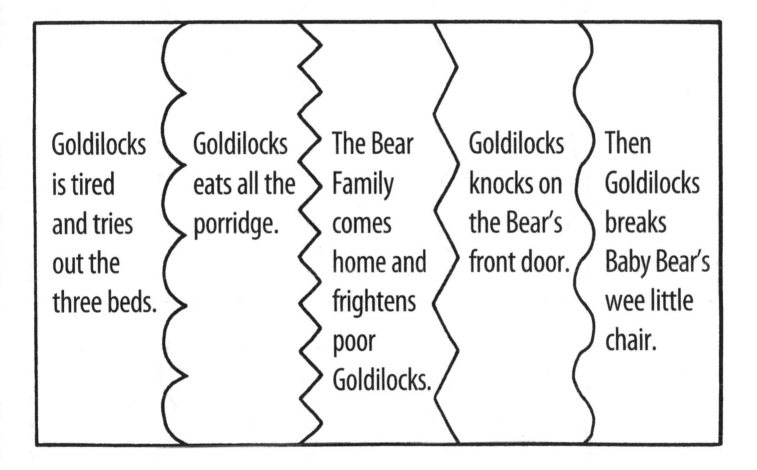

Goldilocks is tired and tries out the three beds.

Goldilocks eats all the porridge.

The Bear Family comes home and frightens poor Goldilocks.

Goldilocks knocks on the Bear's front door.

Then Goldilocks breaks Baby Bear's wee little chair.

Fairy Tale Puzzle Worksheet

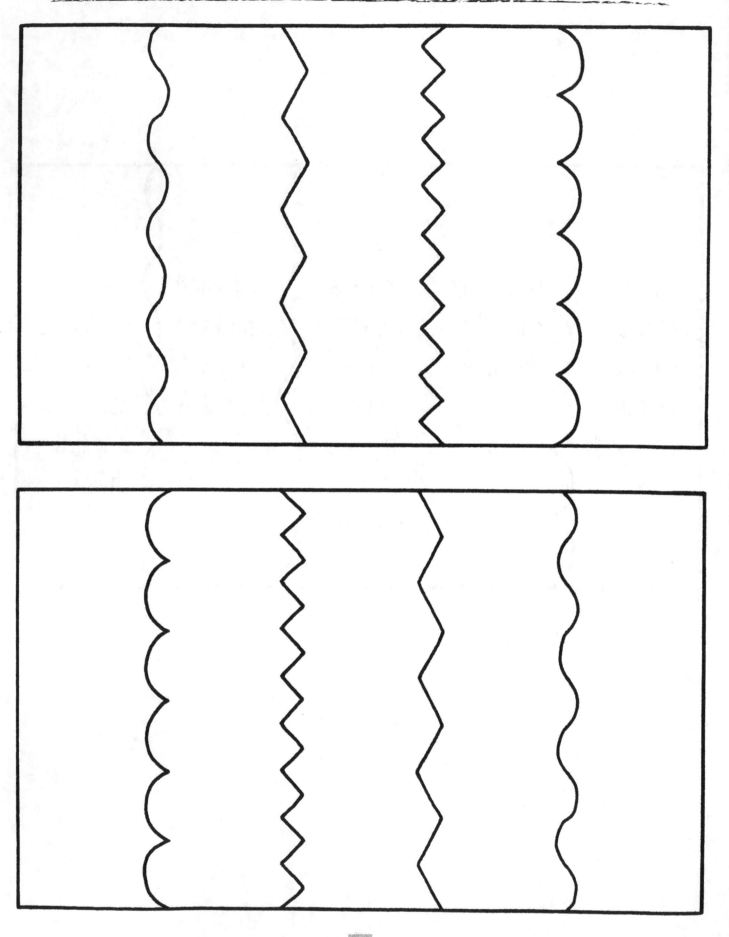

Spy Time
I Spy a Rhyme Time

Benchmarks/Standards covered:
- Identify rhyming words with the same or different spelling patterns.
- Add, delete, or change sounds in a given word to create new or rhyming words.
- Use organizational strategies to play writing.
- Write in complete sentences.

Books to explore:

I Spy School Days: A Book of Picture Riddles by Jean Marzollo and Walter Wick (Scholastic, 1995)

The Scholastic Rhyming Dictionary by Sue Young (Scholastic, 1997)

Where the Sidewalk Ends by Shel Silverstein (HarperCollins, 30th Anniversary Edition, 2004)

Wool Gathering: A Sheep Family Reunion by Lisa Wheeler (Antheneum/Richard Jackson Books, 2001)

Gold Fever by Verla Kay (Putnam Publishing, 1999)

Discussion:

Rhyming words are words that sound the same. Rhymes are fun! Who can give me an example of two words that rhyme? (Allow students to share several examples or share some examples from one of the books listed or another favorite poem or book.) Writers sometimes use rhymes when they're writing a rhyming poem or if they just want to have fun in a story. We're going to be a doing a fun writing activity in just a bit. To help us get started, we need to brainstorm some rhymes. Look around the classroom. Can anyone find two things that rhyme? For example: flag and bag, boy and toy, chair and hair. (Record several rhymes on the board or overhead.)

Now it's your turn:

It looks as if we have a pretty good supply of rhyming words. Let's start our game. It's called I Spy A Rhyme Time. Look around the classroom and find two things that rhyme. Try to think of one we didn't write on the board! Next, write a riddle like this: I spy a flag hanging above a bag. Who spies the flag I'm talking about? You can also write your riddle this way: I spy a boy and a toy. (Write the words "I spy" on the board for reference.) The two things you pick have to be things inside the classroom or things outside the window that everyone can see. Check to see if your words rhyme by reading them out loud. When you're done, bring your riddle up to me. When everyone has finished, we'll read and try to solve them together.

Reminders for student writers:

- Your rhyming words can be proper names if you'd like.
- If you need help with a rhyme, check the rhyming dictionary.
- If you spy *three* things that rhyme, make your Rhyme Time a three-word riddle.

Teaching tips:

- You can challenge students by asking them to extend their riddles. For example, "I spy a flag hanging above a bag. What color is the bag?"

- Allow students to illustrate their riddles. Put all the illustrations together in a collage on a bulletin board and add the riddles below. Let kids play "I Spy" during down times or as a writing center.

- Have students create their own class rhyming wall. Pick a common word and have children brainstorm all the words they can think of that rhyme with it.

Spy Time
What Is It?

Benchmarks/Standards covered:

- Use end punctuation such as exclamation points, question marks, and periods correctly.
- Write labels for objects.
- Illustrate writing samples for display and for sharing with others.

Books to explore:

The Three Questions by Jon J. Muth (Scholastic, 2002)

The Kids' Book of Questions (for ages 9-12 years) by Gregory Stock (Workman Publishing, 1988)

Why? The Best Ever Question and Answer Book About Nature, Science and the World Around You by Catherine Ripley (Maple Tree Press, 2001)

How Things Work: Ask Me a Question: A Picture Flip Quiz for 5-7 Year Olds by Brenda Williams (Miles Kelly Publishing, 2003)

Discussion:

(Begin lesson by bringing out sealed paper bag or gift bag.) Today, we're going to play a guessing game. I've put something in this bag. I will give you clues about what it is by answering your questions. We can keep track of the clues on the board. You can ask me anything except what the object is! (Take students' questions until they have narrowed down the options.) Are you ready to make a guess? (Write down the students' guess in the form of a question. "Is it a _____?" After they've correctly guessed, celebrate and then continue.) Did you notice the punctuation mark I put at the end of my sentence? Because this was a question, I made sure to end the sentence with a question mark.

Now it's your turn:

You're going to get the chance to write your own "What is it?" riddles. (Hand out small gift bags or paper to make into an envelope.) First, think of something to put in your bag. Since we can't put real objects in our bags, we'll have to draw a picture of our mystery object. At the bottom of the drawing, write what it is. Next, think about your object's size, color, shape, use, feel, smell, taste, and then think of at least five clues about your object. For example: it's red; it's something too sweet to eat; it's long and skinny. On another piece of paper, write down your clues.

Reminders for student writers:

- Give your readers at least five clues. (Older students should be able to come up with seven to 10 clues.)

- Don't forget to put your name or initials on your mystery bag.

- Give your readers useful clues. Saying something is smaller than a house isn't very helpful because lots of things are smaller than a house. Saying your mystery item tastes sour is better than just saying you can eat it.

Teaching tips:

- When finished, put the gift bags and clues on display and have students write down a guess. (Remind them to use a question mark. ("Is it a ____?")

- Challenge students to write more (or less) clues depending on their skill level.

- Play 20 Questions when you have a few spare minutes in the classroom.

- Instead of using small gift bags or envelopes, let students wrap their items in pieces of wrapping paper. Ask parents to donate all their scraps or almost-empty rolls of wrapping paper.

Spy Time
Round-Robin Stories

Benchmarks/Standards covered:

- Organize writing to include a beginning, middle, and end.
- Construct complete sentences with subjects and verbs.
- Predict what will happen next, using pictures and content as a guide.

Books to explore:

The Big Bad Rumor by Jonathan Meres (Orchard Books, 2000)
The Secret Knowledge of Grown-ups by David Wisniewski (HarperTrophy, reprint 2001)
The Sky is Falling by Betty Miles (Simon & Schuster, 1998)

Discussion:

(Begin by playing a game of Telephone, the game where you sit in a circle and somebody whispers something to the person next to him or her and it goes around the circle. Afterward, send students back to their seats.) I bet you didn't know it, but we just showed how important it is to have an outline. Writing a story without an outline is like playing Telephone. If you don't know where your story is going, then it's easy for the story to take detours and end up not being what you wanted. On the other hand, sometimes it's a lot of fun to take an unexpected path. Today we're going to do an activity that demonstrates both these points. It's called round-robin writing.

Now it's your turn:

Ready to try writing round-robin style? (Divide students into small groups. See tips.) Each person in your group needs to write a story beginning. Give your story a title, a main character, and a problem for the main character to solve. (After everyone has finished, have them pass their papers to the person to their left.) When you get your neighbor's paper, read the opening paragraph and add to it. You only have a few minutes to work so don't think too much, just write! (After a few minutes, stop students.) This time, I want you to fold the paper so only what you've just written shows. In other words, hide the opening paragraph. Done? *Now* pass the story to the next person. (Continue to have students read and add a few sentences to the stories. Each time, ask them to fold the story so only their work shows before passing it along. Keep passing until the stories make their way back to their original authors. I usually have one student in each group mark the edge of his or her paper with their name in red marker so tracking is easier. After everyone has their story—but before they unfold and read—have them write an ending for the story. Share the stories.)

Reminders for student writers:

- There is one rule for adding to the stories: no violence where a character is seriously injured or killed. Slapstick is okay, though.

- Don't worry about stopping in mid-sentence.

- If you can't read the handwriting of the person before, you can quietly ask him or her what he or she wrote.

Teaching tips:

- Bigger groups mean crazier stories, but you don't want to do as many passes as there are students. Younger students may feel too overwhelmed. Groups of four to eight students work well.

- Use the "no violence" rule. If you don't, students may elect to "kill off" the main character each time he or she writes; this makes it very difficult for the following person to continue the stories.

- The results of this activity are usually hysterical. Be sure to save plenty of time to share.

- It is also fun to have the original author create a cartoon with illustrations for the events in the story. This can be done in the computer lab in KidPix® or a drawing program.

Index

About the Author

Carmella Van Vleet earned a degree in Elementary Education with emphasis in Language Arts and Early Childhood from Emporia State University. She taught kindergarten for several years before becoming an instructor at the Thurber Writing Academy, a community program in Columbus, Ohio that brings together students and writers. She is the author of numerous books for children as well as *Writing Club: A Year of Writing Workshops for Grades 2-5* and *How to Handle School Snafus*. She lives near Columbus, Ohio with her husband and their three children.